Paul Franklin B.Ed. (Hons) is a retired headteacher after twenty-five years in the profession. All of his work has been drawn from life experiences, with each of his poems or songs having an anecdotal backdrop. Over the years, his pupils, staff and family have provided the necessary approval for the subject matter of his printed work.

I would like to dedicate *Three in a Bed* to partnerships of lifelong love, commitment and dedication.

The contents of this book are entirely true.
For those individuals who may dispute its validity due to memory loss or embarrassment,
Reg advises them to get over it!

Paul Franklin

# THREE IN A BED

AUSTIN MACAULEY PUBLISHERS
LONDON · CAMBRIDGE · NEW YORK · SHARJAH

Copyright © Paul Franklin 2024

The right of Paul Franklin to be identified as author of this work has been asserted by the author in accordance with sections 77 and 78 of the Copyright, Designs and Patents Act 1988.

All rights reserved. No part of this publication may be reproduced, stored in a retrieval system, or transmitted in any form or by any means, electronic, mechanical, photocopying, recording, or otherwise, without the prior permission of the publishers.

Any person who commits any unauthorised act in relation to this publication may be liable to criminal prosecution and civil claims for damages.

All of the events in this memoir are true to the best of the author's memory. The views expressed in this memoir are solely those of the author.

A CIP catalogue record for this title is available from the British Library.

ISBN 9781035883882 (Paperback)
ISBN 9781035883899 (ePub e-book)

www.austinmacauley.com

First Published 2024
Austin Macauley Publishers Ltd®
1 Canada Square
Canary Wharf
London
E14 5AA

# Chapter One

"Hello Reg. How are you? I heard that you had received some sad news. Am I correct in thinking that your brother has died?"

"I hope so, they've just planted him!"

The woman's face recoiled, rather like an inflated balloon being pulled back by its knotted neck between the index and middle fingers, prior to release. Etched into her face was a look of confusion, discomfort and embarrassment. The question was delivered sensitively enough, but the reply was typical of my father's irreverential behaviour. He has always remained quick-witted and humorous. Honestly, trying to get a serious word out of him is like Donald Trump trying to hold down his comb-over in a high wind!

Dick had indeed passed on. Born in 1931, Reg was one of *fifteen* children. His father had brought ten boys and five girls into this world, through two marriages. His mother also miscarried twins and lost another little girl aged three.

The 1911 census records my grandfather's occupation as 'head ploughman' on a farm in Bushey Mill Lane, Watford, which became a reserved occupation in the Great War. Ironically, he didn't see action, but six of his boys did in

World War II and what is more surprising, unlike Private Ryan's siblings, they all returned home safely.

Reg told me that his father was a farmhand during the day, but also worked hard at night.

"Oh," I said. "What other work was he involved in?"

"Well, he did have fifteen children!" was his cheeky reply. "My mum walked like John Wayne coming through bat-wing doors!"

As well as a modest income from the farm work, my grandfather received favourable rewards from catching indigenous crayfish from the River Colne which flowed past the bottom of his garden. He would then pack these in wet sacks to keep them alive and send them by train to the top chefs in London, who would pay him premium rates. His entrepreneurial skills were never in doubt, but the financial benefits from his enterprising endeavours were wasted on alcohol.

His horticultural skills were as legendary as his imbibing. He often grew prize-winning vegetables, which were the talk of competitive shows. Once he won thirty awards in one show! Reg recalls how, on one occasion, his father gave a friend some 'First Prize' carrots to take home and cook for his family. Instead, he entered them into another show, where they won again! When the news got back to him my grandfather was less than amused. One can't help but admire such opportunistic tendencies, in much the same way as my grandfather's tax-free, freshwater harvests, but even so, this so-called friend ended up with prize-winning 'cauliflower ears' when they next met!

My grandmother worked hard to make ends meet. Reg loved her and sacrificed his schooling to work in a brewery by the age of fifteen, to bring in an income to help her.

When Reg's eldest brother Alf, returned from the war, he applied for and secured himself a job as a labourer, working on the construction of the A41. He was a proud man and would journey to and from his construction site in a *three-piece suit and bowler hat*, before changing into and out of his working overalls. This level of sartorial self-respect is redolent of a by-gone age, such as the arrival of Caribbean passengers aboard the Windrush and vastly different from the likes of Dominic Cummings who disregarded formal codes of attire, by entering Number 10 dressed like a homeless person, wearing lost-property clothing. It certainly lends weight to his excuse for jumping in a car at Barnard Castle to test his eyesight during the COVID-19 pandemic because he can't be seeing what the rest of us are when he looks in the mirror!

## Chapter Two

It's true to suggest that my father is legendary in his part of the world, for being an outstanding darts player. He still plays competitive matches to this day as a nonagenarian!

On numerous occasions, he represented his town or county in regional or national competitions.

Admittedly, he's had to shift his preference for the treble twenty bed to treble nineteen at the bottom of the board because he can't raise his arm easily now. What's more remarkable is that his skills were forged from a young age, in a family where *everyone* played to a high standard. His family had their own darts team and went on tour playing exhibition matches. Whenever a game was in session, it was a serious affair. If music was still playing at the onset, a look from one of the brothers to the publican would be enough to curtail it. Their reputation preceded them and the interest of onlookers was palpable.

In our earlier years, when my brother Pete and I accompanied our father on gardening jobs, we would often stop at a pub on the way home for a drink and a practice session on the board.

On one such occasion, Reg was about to throw his darts when a short, balding fellow walked across his line of sight.

Both Pete and I grimaced as we wondered how Reg would respond; and respond he did, by following this chap around the room, slapping the top of his head, as in a Benny Hill sketch, whilst 'tutting' to the beat of each slap and sounding out staccato instructions, "Don't... walk... across... my... line... of... sight!"

How he managed to persuade this gentleman to play 'doubles' after his humiliation is anyone's guess, but I suspect it was pure intimidation. Expectedly, he also directed the publican to turn off the music! Once established in one of his own locals, the music went off as soon as he took his darts out of their wooden case.

Years ago, I remember entering a pub called the Railway Inn, by the Bushey Arches on the outskirts of Watford where I noticed an old photograph featuring darts players above the bar. On the left-hand side of the teams' board in the picture, every player's name on the home team was 'Franklin'. There were two sets of twins on the other side; interesting, but not nearly as impressive. My grandfather was holding the cup they had just won. Reg's recollection of that match was that during the whole team leg of that game, involving 'one-thousand-and-one up', no player on his family side, required a second visit to the 'oche'. Every 'singles' match was also won.

Playing darts in the Franklin family was almost a religious observance. Practice and rivalry amongst the siblings were rife. The girls also took the game seriously. Reg's late sister Sheila played for Essex and once beat 'The Crafty Cockney' Eric Bristow at the time he was ranked the world's no. 1.

Reg and his older brothers Fred and Ken would often play exhibition darts at the King Harry pub in St Albans and although their routine was well-rehearsed, it involved some very unsettling and disturbing, if not reckless showmanship. On frequent occasions, as a finale, each of the boys would take it in turn to stand directly beneath the 'bull', partially covering the 'twenty-five' ring and facing the thrower, as he threw a dart from eight feet through their hair and into the 'fifty' or outer ring.

This 'William Tell' party piece would most certainly never pass muster with today's health and safety guidelines, but neither should it have at that time! They were mad; unequivocally brave and supremely confident, but nevertheless, bloody mad! Unbelievably, Reg once challenged a confident dart player to attempt the shot above his head. All he remembers is an overwhelming sense of dread as this stranger sweated profusely and missed the target by two feet into the wall. Reg says he doesn't know who was more nervous and the offer never went out again.

It's hard to believe the brothers also threw sharpened, four-inch nails in matches!

"What possessed you to do that?" I once asked.

"Because we could!" was his immodest reply.

This flagrant breach of safety went on for some considerable time until inevitably someone got injured. My Uncle Ken threw a heavily weighted dart and during one such 'show' a misdirected 'mini-missile' entered my father's scalp, beneath the hairline and embedded itself into his skull! Reg remembers a crimson carpet of red blood cells suddenly appearing from the sharp, painful impact, covering his eyes.

This part of the exhibition was subsequently, though unsurprisingly dropped from the act.

One might say the fine margins of error, in this case, make the job of a knife-thrower's assistant seem a better option. In either case, it can only be one step down from facing a firing squad. What springs to mind with this attitude of carefree abandon to personal safety, is the notion that one doesn't need a parachute to make a parachute jump... but it *is* vital to make a second attempt!

The whole exercise certainly sounded at the least risky, if not potentially life-threatening.

My father's obsession and overwhelming urge to be the best in his game saw him achieve an extraordinary feat, that even to this day I have never forgotten and deserves admiration. During my studies for a degree in teaching, he suffered a debilitating attack of dartitis. He suffered a very real psychological problem with his technique and the release of his darts that seriously affected his performance. Any normal person would have probably succumbed to the inevitable struggle and given up, or at least waited for it to show signs of improvement. However, he wasn't prepared to let it defeat him and so embarked on a long period of intense training to learn how to throw with his left hand! He would practise up to *six* or sometimes *eight* hours a day to perfect throwing with his weaker limb. Up early before work, during lunchtimes and in the evenings, the practice was relentless.

As praiseworthy as indeed this was, there were times when the 'thud-thud-thud' of his practice drove us all mad; me especially, as his old elm-board in the kitchen was directly beneath my bedroom, where I was trying to study. The darts incessantly and inexorably pounded into the target with a precise rhythm, like Chinese water torture. At times, the expected rhythm and flow of the darts were interrupted by an aggravating pause, as his sightline was obscured by an odd-angled flight, causing him to move to the left or right before releasing the next dart: Thud, thud, followed by an agonizing wait, then eventually… thud! I lost count of the pencils I snapped in my hand and mouth, as this torment unfolded over time.

Nevertheless and quite remarkably, he got to a level of competence with his 'wrong' hand to enable him to resume competitive matches. Amazingly, he found himself in a county-level competition match in Park Street St Albans, which he disappointingly lost after winning the first set.

I was standing at the bar at the end of the game when Reg's unsuspecting though triumphant opponent came up to his team captain standing next to me and said, "So that was the famous Reg Franklin that I've heard so much about. He didn't put up that much of a contest, did he?"

His captain replied, "Why don't you invite him to another game and play with your left hand."

"Why? I'm right-handed."

"So is he, but he gave you a good run for your money with his other hand. Now go and buy *him* a drink."

The expression on his opponent's face was one of incredulity and one I shall never forget.

Reg always had an air of mischief about him and during one closely contested match at his local, put his hand into his pocket to retrieve some chalk, whilst intentionally giving the impression that he had accidentally dropped a folded £5 note. One of the oppositions noticed this and surreptitiously took possession of it, unaware that it was a ruse. He immediately went to the bar, ordered a round of drinks for himself and his teammates and handed the folded note to the publican, who in turn said, "I think you'll find this note belongs to Reg Franklin."

"No," he said claiming ownership, "It's definitely mine."

"Oh, then how do you explain what's written on it—I promise never to pay the bearer who nicked this £5 note? We've got another one here Reg!"

"That'll teach the thieving bastard!"

Reg was always generous to a fault and often exploited where money was concerned, especially when he worked as a gardener in later years. He abhorred the Ebenezer Scrooge types who found it hard to part with their money. Of his many brothers-in-law, he identified one in particular who revealed such a trait and always capitalised on any occasion to relieve him of his 'stash'.

I remember at a family wedding, Reg was at the bar buying a large round that he couldn't afford, when my uncle waltzed over to him, never wanting to miss the chance of a free drink. Rather than pay bar prices, he had even brought his own drinks to the event! Aware of his intentions, Reg finished ordering all the drinks he wanted, including his own and then asked 'Buff' (short for buffalo breath—he suffered from acute halitosis) what he wanted, "That's very kind of you Reg, I'll have a double brandy."

"Of course, you will… and a double brandy please barman, and he's kindly paying for this round (pointing at his shocked, surprised and wrong-footed brother-in-law who has now attracted the grateful thanks of all around.) Thanks, Buff, much appreciated."

Extracting himself from the scene (of a crime, in my uncle's view I suppose) Reg fist-pumped the air and watched as 'Buff' was enveloped by the hordes of grateful family members and obviously unable to back out of the unintentional philanthropic act. In those days, twenty-four pounds was a lot of money, and it took Buff a long time to get over the shock!

I played with and partnered with Reg in league matches from the tender age of fourteen. His team's home pub was The Red Lion directly opposite Watford's football ground.

On frequent occasions, but in one memorable game he left me a double to win a league match, "Nothing to worry about son, double-four is a good bed."

The first attempt narrowly missed the wire and landed in the four. The second landed in the two. Then came the whisper in my ear, "You can do this, son. Hit it on the up, but don't miss… I'm standing right under the bull."

No pressure then! The moisture evaporated in my mouth before I dry-swallowed and focused on double-one. The silence was shattering and the expectations were onerous. Then, as if it were a laser beam, the dart impacted with the board in the correct bed. Up went the roar! One of the team ordered a brandy.

I'd never had one before, not least of all because I was well underage! The spirit burned the back of my throat and made me cough and splutter; much to the delight and excitement of onlookers. Their inappropriate though humorous outbursts rang in my ears, but the occasion made me realise and appreciate the buzz that Reg got from winning.

"Nice one son, we'll make a darts player of you yet!" He didn't, but what he successfully achieved, was to embed in me and my future children, the desire to succeed.

Many years later, when I moved to West Yorkshire, I joined a local darts team that practised on a Friday night, more for the social aspect than serious competition. On the rare occasions when Reg and Ruth came to stay with us, I took him down to my local for a game. When Reg revealed his talents (his mental arithmetic and preferred numerical permutations for any given total were equally incredible) the team wanted to sign him up immediately.

Reg politely declined giving 'distance to travel' as a genuine excuse. The captain, however, still signed him up, stating that he would be welcome to play in any match. To a man, each member offered to give up their place, should he turn up unexpectedly. Praise indeed!

It would be months if not years before Reg returned, as I would more often travel south to see him, but when he did, the team's long-standing agreement was invoked and all players willingly offered to step down, to allow him to represent them. Only one of those players is still alive and on the rare occasion I bump into him, he still respectfully asks after Reg and would dearly love to see him again. How the passage of time inevitably brings equal amounts of joy and sadness, with the reviving of fond memories and irretrievable moments.

As stated, my father's competitive nature was eventually passed down to us as kids. Like any proud parent, Reg and Ruth invested a lot of time in the belief of their children's destinies, and this commendable outlook has undoubtedly been and will be passed down to grandchildren and great-grandchildren. For example, my sisters Claire and Barbara trained hard to be swimmers, specialising in speed and stamina disciplines respectively.

Claire eventually made it to a high standard, competing in international events and representing her country only to be devastated by a serious back injury in training, which prevented her from continuing. Notwithstanding, her sense of discipline and commitment was ingrained into her sons; one of whom called Will, at the time of writing has a contract with Bournemouth F.C. as a goalkeeper and has been on loan to Kilmarnock.

Barbara swam with the grace of a dolphin and after long periods of training in the Thames along with the constant threat of infection by Weil's disease, swam the Channel in 1978; no mean feat, even in an age which now sees swimmers perform multiple crossings.

Reg says he persuaded her to do it because he couldn't afford the ticket for her passage to France.

My younger brother Peter once took part in a relay swim of the Channel, organised and attended by Sir Douglas Bader, the Battle of Britain air ace. Upon meeting him in the hotel lift and much to the astonishment and wasted pleas of my brother, Reg asked Bader if he was going to take his shoes, socks and *legs* off and get involved. Bader smiled and intimated that even with air/sea rescue on standby, he had always been reluctant to do so and anyway, the water would put out his pipe!

At the same event and to the lasting dismay of Pete, Reg met the two team leaders—the great Henry Cooper and Joe Bugner—and asked them if they wanted a fight… with each other, not him!

Like darts, I didn't pursue swimming, due to the overwhelming fear and belief instilled in me since the release of 'Jaws', that something with teeth appearing out of the depths, would rip my arse off! Dad, quite rightly, said it was an irrational fear where indoor pools were concerned, and I would be more likely to catch myself in the teeth of my zip, whilst getting changed; every bit as painful I'm sure, but not life-threatening.

# Chapter Three

As was the case back then, Reg followed his siblings into the army by virtue of the mandatory enlistment of people into national service or 'conscription' as it was called. Reg had his own interpretation and called it 'legal press-ganging'. And so, in 1949, at the tender age of eighteen, he was initially assigned to the Royal Army Service Corps, before serving as a 'red cap' or military policeman in occupied Germany for two years. He underwent extensive motorbike and jeep training, often extolling the virtues of Norton motorcycles; a company that sadly went into administration, but fortunately has returned under new ownership.

For the most part, he enjoyed his time in the army, earning himself a reputation amongst the ranks for being an honourable and trustworthy non-commissioned officer. Indeed, on many occasions, he overlooked the late returns of soldiers on short leave and often waived the rulebook on minor indiscretions. These qualities earned him a great deal of respect. However, on one occasion, Reg had worked hard to prepare his vehicle for V.I.P. escort duty, in readiness for the arrival of Aneurin Bevan (Nye) who was at that time, the appointed Minister of Health and responsible for establishing the National Health Service.

On the night before the MP's visit, Reg drove to a nearby army camp to play in a darts match he had organised. Upon his return to the jeep, he was shocked to see that it had been vandalised. Crestfallen and feeling betrayed, he worked all night to rectify the damage.

That following week saw a marked change in his attitude towards leniency. He was far less patient or tolerant of soldiers' misdemeanours and took a much harder line on discipline. In fact, he embarked upon a rampage of retribution.

This contrast prompted his associates to ask why. As a result of their investigations, a new batch of recruits were found to be responsible and severely dealt with. Normal services were shortly resumed.

Reg's unorthodox showing of compassion and benevolence towards others as far as regulations were concerned, attracted much criticism and disapproval from his Sergeant Major, who was always trying to put *him* on a charge. Despite relentless determination, he was never successful. Men would even bet on Reg's ability to overturn any charges brought against him. In one case, the Sergeant Major had written a report to be read out at a hearing, accusing him of failing in his duty on the 31$^{st}$ of a given month. When the commanding officer asked if the indictment was true, my father replied, "Well, obviously not, there are only thirty days in that month."

The charges were subsequently dropped, much to the amusement of the attendees, with the exception of the plaintiff who continued his vendetta to no avail, rather like the continual battle of wits between 'Wile E. Coyote' and the 'Roadrunner'.

Incidentally, we always comment on how Dad laughs uncontrollably out loud at the antics of the latter pair, 'Tom and Jerry', 'Elmer Fudd' and 'Bugs Bunny' or 'Laurel and Hardy'. When asked why, he simply says, "It reminds me of my long-suffering Sergeant Major, the poor bastard!"

# Chapter Four

In 1950, Reg got a job at Odhams, the printworks in Watford on the A41 with his brother George. It was there he met my mother Ruth working in the phone office. Reg says it was love at first sight, "Well, it was for me anyhow. Your mother took a little longer to be convinced."

I'm not at all surprised. His opening gambit was an inspired, epic one-liner, "Do you like darts?"

She's had years to regret her answer—all seventy-one of them!

"Honestly, son, we've been inseparable; we've done everything together, and I take her everywhere I go… that way I don't have to kiss her goodbye!"

Then winking cheekily, laughs out loud.

After a whirlwind romance (his words), they got married in 1953, the year of the coronation. Reg says their event was more memorable and so it should have been for several reasons; not least of all because it was a double ceremony, with his brother Ken marrying Molly, my mother's sister, who actually turned out to be her mother! Unbelievably, Ruth was delivered this huge bombshell on the eve of their wedding!

Can you imagine the scenario? Throughout childhood and adulthood, believing this person to be your sister, sharing secrets and intimate details, in a way one wouldn't with one's mother and then at the age of twenty, your world is turned upside down with a confession from which you'll never fully recover. On top of this, you must convince everyone at the ceremony, the *next* day that it's the best day of your life! Reg says he told Ruth over the phone, "If you're going to wake up with a smile on your face tomorrow, you'll have to put a coat hanger in your mouth before you go to bed tonight."

Shockingly, though hardly surprisingly, Reg fell asleep on his wedding night after drinking almost non-stop throughout the day. In the early hours of the following morning, he turned over and sensing the presence of someone else in the bed, asked them what they were doing there. Ruth replied, "I really don't know."

Back in the day, the perceived disgrace single mothers attracted to their families forced parents to concoct alternative explanations for their children's indiscretions and so my grandmother was *blessed* with another sister, which she presumably found out about after her protracted sojourn to a distant place.

We tried, right up to her deathbed to learn who our maternal grandfather was, but to no avail. It may have been out of embarrassment—rape was always a consideration, but so was a possible fling with a passing sailor! That at least would explain my sisters' love of the water.

Sadly, we shall never know, but we've spent some long hours speculating and debating the subject as well as laughing over some of the hypotheses. A royal bloodline was considered, but only by my father, as this idea would have elevated his standing. In truth, if Molly was never going to reveal these details, then it would have probably been better not to have known anything, especially for our mother's sake. She never *really* forgave her.

The pain didn't end there either. Within eight years of marriage, Molly lost Ken who succumbed to bowel cancer after spending months nursing him. Life at times can be cruel.

Reg felt the loss keenly. He makes no secret of the fact that Ken was his closest brother. He had served as a Red Beret towards the end of the war. Looking through his personal possessions, Dad showed me his combat dagger. I distinctly remember it having notches on the handle.

The likely relevance of this record-keeping didn't resonate with me until I was much older. However, my limited experiences with and memories of Uncle Ken, convince me that not only was he a man who loved his family, but was also extremely kind and caring; possibly unlike my Uncle Fred who would hand out Christmas cards at a family funeral to save on postal costs. He was just practical-minded and sometimes didn't think, just like the time he decided to name his first child Lord Mark, which would require some explanation.

Fred was a lover of cricket and so decided to call his son after the founder of the home of English cricket. The transposition of this exercise didn't quite work; not least of all because 'Lord' was the founder's surname. Nevertheless, Mark was certainly going to try and benefit as well as receive abuse from his nomenclature. Unfortunately, he often lacked the judgement or commitment to see any deception through to its end. Such as the time he was in a bar capitalising on the generosity and misguided reverence of other unsuspecting customers, thinking he was a real member of the aristocracy when he decided to share the real origin of his name. His ejection from the premises was ignominious, not to say extremely uncomfortable. Unbelievable! His preferred adornment of a 'deerstalker' only served to reinforce people's misconceived ideas. Reg often told him that he should drop the name 'Lord' for the more apposite title of 'Skid'. We found this amusing; I'm guessing Lord Mark less so!

# Chapter Five

Angling is among the number of water sports pursued by my family and none of whom is more passionate towards it, or indeed more authoritative on the subject than Ruth. She has won as many competitions and trophies in her pastime as Reg has in darts and certainly more than him in freshwater fishing. What is more extraordinary is that she became interested and indeed proficient at it, even at a time when it was considered unusual for women to be so.

When I was researching the book, I asked Dad at which point during their marriage did Mum become 'hooked' as it were, on her hobby, "When I allowed her to hold my rod son—my fishing rod that is," he said in his inimitable way. Of course, no clarification was required, but he offered it nonetheless because he loves puns and double entendres.

All I could think of at the time was a quote from the late, great Ronnie Barker, "The marvellous thing about a joke with a double meaning is that it can only mean one thing." How true.

They became life members of two clubs, both in which Ruth was the only female and fished countless others as guests in competitions. She was greatly respected and admired by the male fraternity, including the notoriously competitive carp fishermen, a good number of whom she beat convincingly. She was frequently mentioned in and won prizes from the 'Angling Times' in their section for 'Catch of the Week'.

I occasionally, though sometimes reluctantly, accompanied my parents to their lake and river at weekends and during the holidays, as I had little interest in fishing. What I found hard to understand, was how anyone could remain motionless for most of the day, sometimes in the most abominable weather and frequently catch bugger all! A bit like cricket perhaps, but I like cricket! For a youngster, it is hard to accept that live bait, by which I mean maggots (Mum calls them gentles) are stored in the fridge next to the food we eat! Even more unappealing, if not sickening, is the horrifying fact that she casually popped them in her mouth to warm them up, before impaling them on her hook.

Now, as an older and wiser person, I've come to appreciate that maggots have been extremely beneficial in the advancement of medical science. Even so, the sight of them now sitting next to my egg mayonnaise sandwiches is still disconcerting, but back in the day, it was horrifying! There were even times I'll have you know, when my mother forgot she had left an open box of bait at the bottom of her tackle box during the closed season, only to be reminded when the house was filled with the angry buzzing of metamorphosed 'gentles' into blue-arsed flies!

During the hot weather, hanging keep nets would stink like decaying fish and once my parents brought a 17lb (8 kg in new money) pike home to eat! It tasted like soil, but moreover, it frightened the cat—inducing pet P.T.S.D.—out of its wits when the latter jumped up onto the bath, only to be faced with a head of wide-open eyes and mouth, full of menacing teeth.

The hardest part of all for me and Dad was trying to get Mum to pack up and come home, especially if she'd had a particularly unrewarding day.

For hours, I would sit and eat incalculable amounts of sandwiches, crisps and chocolate and read *Commando* book war stories and *Victor* comics, whilst my mother sat stock-still, transfixed on her tiny bobbing float, willing it to be pulled under, by some unsuspecting tench or bream.

Once, my boredom was alleviated by my feeding a passing rat which subsequently scuttled over Mum's feet, perversely, causing her to suddenly cry out in shock, eventually settling down and ironically placing more cold maggots in her mouth before torturing them to death!

Contrarily, to witness the compassionate way, she caught, held and released fish, was a sight to behold. She would talk to them softly and after weighing, hold them in her hands, gently thrusting them forward under the water, to allow it to pass through their gills, enriching their oxygen levels before releasing.

'And away' as recited by Paul Whitehouse and Bob Mortimer in 'Gone Fishing'. This level of benevolence was never extended to us as teenagers, I jokingly state, as I can't remember Mum cooking us a Sunday roast, on account of her never being at home. From a positive point of view, we eventually did learn how to cook, but not before consuming an unhealthy amount of 'Shiphams' fish and meat paste.

However, as we all succeeded in our own individual endeavours, we certainly valued the way she became committed to her sport with great resilience and application.

One doesn't become a respected sportsperson, by constantly cooking, cleaning and ironing for others. She had performed enough of those duties when we were younger.

Whilst Ruth was building her reputation as a competitive and successful angler, Reg worked hard to develop skills which only reinforced others' opinions of his socially unacceptable tendencies.

Often, across the quiet stillness and sun-dappled surface of the lake, with the calm lapping of the water, gently kissing the banks and occasional flapping of iridescent insect wings amongst the waving flora, would come a thunderous ear-splitting, silence-shattering, earth-quaking explosion of a bowl-emission. This would be followed by the angry admonishments of members in other swims, often a good distance from himself:

"For God's sake, Reg, you're disturbing the fish."

It wasn't just the fish… huge flocks of birds would be spooked and taken to the air in alarm.

To say the volume of these eruptions was notable is flirting recklessly with the understatement, but the resulting bellow of laughter was just as disturbing, "Sorry, was that too loud?"

A normally unwelcomed reputation preceded him, but inexplicably, Reg courted and played up to this infamous recognition.

Fast forward fifteen or so years later, I was driving in my tiny Ford Fiesta to Wall Hall Teacher Training College, between Radlett and Watford. As I momentarily stopped to turn right into the college grounds, there was a bone-crushing collision from behind, which caused me to lose consciousness. Eventually, as I came around, I was aware of a fireman cutting away the driver's door with a power device. The whole car had concertinaed under the impact, thus confining me to a tiny space, with the side of my face thrust against the steering wheel, which in turn had come to a union with the windscreen.

When I finally became extracted from the wreck, all three emergency services were on the scene. The car had been struck from behind by a woman at the wheel of a Volvo estate, who had turned her head prior to the accident, to try and stop her young children from squabbling. The force of the impact had catapulted my car over fifty metres down and across the main road, into a ditch and luckily not into the path of an oncoming vehicle. How I managed to stand on my own two feet after the event is remarkable. The assisting firefighter said that the driver's seat had been completely torn out of the floor which, was probably responsible for saving my life.

After regaining my composure, to a degree, an officer stated that the woman involved had claimed responsibility. The policeman said they were going to charge her under 'dangerous driving' offences and would I like to bring my own charges. Looking at the surrounding carnage of debris, amongst which I spotted pieces of children's artwork, I declined saying that I did not want to add to the woman's obvious anguish. I was young and inexperienced and hadn't realised that the subsequent and possibly huge, not to mention justifiable financial settlement for my psychological injuries, would have come from insurers:

"Are you quite sure?" said the policeman.
"Yes, she's had enough to contend with."
"Well, *we* still are!" said the officer.

Next came the comforting tones from the ambulance driver, who strongly advised that I be transported to the hospital for a serious check-up, "That won't be necessary, thank you. Strangely, I feel fine physically. No bones appear to be broken, and I must hand this dissertation into the college, before the deadline."

"Well, OK then, I'm sure the police will organise the recovery of this wreckage, but what is your name?"

"It's Paul, Paul Franklin."

"Paul Fr... wait a minute, are you Reg Franklin's... are you Farter Franklin's son?"

And to my astonishment and infinite embarrassment, in front of all in attendance, including the woman who caused this horror, he demonstrably hoicked up his leg and supplemented his actions with an unnecessary vocal accompaniment: 'Brrrrrr, brrrrur, brruurrr'. Incredulously, I looked upon his vaudeville entertainment, with more shock than the accident had left me with, as other members of the emergency services howled with laughter.

As the laughter eventually subsided, the paramedic announced, "I know your dad well. I only live four doors down from your house. I'm his darts partner."

"He's an amazing player, but my God, can he fart!" More laughter ensued, much to my alarm and the woman's consternation.

"How are you getting home? I'd take you, but I'm still on an emergency call."

"It's OK; we'll get him back," said a female police officer giggling, "I should like to meet his father."

It was too far for me to walk, but I would have much preferred to have done so.

I have never let my father forget the ignominy of this hugely embarrassing sideshow, though every time I do, he disbelievingly swells with pride and happily recounts the heights of infamy that his derriere, derring-do antics catapulted him to.

Talking of catapulting, this was an effective way of projecting bait to a preferred spot of the angler's swim to attract fish from outside the area. This was a permissible and accepted method of encouragement, even during competitions. Unfortunately, no restrictions were placed on the user or prohibition issued to particular individuals. So Dad loved using it!

Grey squirrels would often blatantly steal food from under the noses of anglers, so once Dad said he would bring some hazelnuts to distract them. When, on this occasion, I walked from Mum's swim to his, (she would never let him fish too close by) I asked how he was doing, "Oddly, I've found out that squirrels don't like hazelnuts as much as everyone thinks."

"Oh really, I thought they loved them?"

"Clearly not, as I've just fed a hazelnut cluster to one attempting to nick my lunch, via a catapult, and it didn't seem too keen at first!"

"Oh, really, what do you mean 'at first'?"

"Well, son, I wasn't trying to hit him, just offering an alternative. They flew over his head and dispersed in the bushes. He then changed his mind and scuttled about collecting them whilst I ate my sandwich. Fussy little thing."

To tell the truth, there were unforeseen and genuine accidents on the lake at times such as a Canada goose flying unexpectedly into the launch of a bait ball; falling motionless onto the water, whereupon the entire resident wildlife appeared to fall silent. Or the time a fish died after the attempted extraction of a hook that it had taken too far down. Quite often lines were cut when the procedure was considered too dangerous.

Thankfully, these occasions were rare but left a lasting impression of remorse on all of us. We were all extremely happy to hear of lead weights and barbed hooks being outlawed. This not only led to the expediency of hook retraction from the fish but also ourselves; both third-party or self-inflicted entanglements.

To his credit, Dad would often attend work parties to clear swims by cutting back foliage or by cutting down rotting or dangerous trees. Not so creditable, was his tendency to contract this unrewarding work out to me. Nevertheless, one Sunday, he drove me to the lake to help him gather up some variable-sized logs that he had cut up, to be transported some distance by punt to the entrance of the club. There, we were to transfer them to the van to be taken home.

It was a bitterly cold morning, so I adorned myself with a beautifully hand-knitted, roll-neck, Arun jumper, which was one of several I had been given by a wonderfully generous woman called Eileen White. They are extremely expensive to buy and interestingly, each of the stitch patterns has a particular meaning. For example, the 'cable' stitch, is said to represent a fisherman's rope; the 'diamond' stitch symbolises the small fields on the islands; the 'zig-zag' stitch represents the inevitable highs and lows of marriage life; the 'honeycomb' stitch is used to represent the hard work and rewards of the bee and the 'trellis' pattern recalls the stonewalled fields of the farming communities. It was a thing of beauty, and I felt proud to wear it.

We had to walk all the way to the top end of the lake, where the punt was waiting. We launched the craft into the water and coiled the tethering rope onto the flat front end. I was then instructed to carefully ensconce myself within its shallow body, whilst Reg carefully surrounded me with the cut logs.

Throughout the process, Reg took care to remind me that we (*we*) shouldn't overload the boat's capacity and that I should be mindful of not rowing too earnestly to avoid becoming swamped with water flowing over the prow. As I tentatively set off, with a strong feeling of trepidation, initiated by Reg's disregard for his own pertinent advice, I was acutely aware of water creeping over the end. As instructed, I rowed with the intention of causing the least amount of disturbance to the surrounding water.

Within fifteen or twenty minutes, I found myself in the centre of the lake, with Reg or indeed anyone for that matter, nowhere in sight. Then, as if to confirm my own self-fulfilling prophecy, the water started to ingress. At first, I calmly accepted this unfolding calamity, but as the icy, cold water started to envelop me, my composure quickly broke down and was replaced with abject panic! My frantic calls for assistance resonated across the early morning mill-pond surface.

I must have yelled at the top of my voice for a good number of minutes, until finally, the punt disappeared from beneath me, and I found myself swimming frantically for the bank. The cold shocked me into a panicked swim to safety but as one might expect, the weight of my woollen jumper seriously hampered my progress.

Having eventually heard my pleas for help, Reg was waiting for me with a concerned look on his face, not for me of course but for the obvious loss of the boat and its contents.

As I slowly emerged from the water, with floating logs everywhere on its surface providing the backdrop, Dad very quickly and considerately enquired as to the whereabouts of the punt.

"It's on the end of this," I said as I handed him the lengthy, uncoiled rope attached to it. He promptly began pulling it in.

As I looked down upon my filthy, soaked Arun, to my utter consternation I realised that the weight of the water it absorbed, had stretched the garment to the dimensions of a ball gown!

On top of this calamity and the ensuing discomfort I was experiencing, we had to go through the entire process once again, until we had retrieved all the logs which had broken free of their confinement.

The journey home can be described at best as wet, miserable and uncomfortable, with the necessary unloading of the logs in the back garden as intolerable.

When Ruth saw the state of me, she made an admirable effort to save the jumper, washing it by hand and then sandwiching it between two large towels. The outcome was a classy roll-neck that would have perfectly fitted my 'Action Man'.

# Chapter Six

As children, up until our teens, we regularly went to the west country for our holidays. On several earlier occasions, we camped or caravanned in Dorset at a place called 'Durdle Door'. I remember during one break here as young children, we were aware that Dad was uncharacteristically sombre, but he nevertheless remained committed to giving us a memorable time. He would often take us to the beach for a swim or exploratory walk, usually investigating rock pools. On some occasions, the Atlantic could be very cold (we never had wet suits in those days) and my 'crown jewels' were reduced to a size that one might find within a watch movement.

We never had a miserable or unexciting time during this period, and it wasn't until much later that we learnt from Mum that Reg had lost his father, but had decided to miss the funeral in order to ensure that his family were not disappointed, by having to return home earlier than expected.

Later, we were to camp for nine years in succession at a place called Trevornick at Holywell Bay near Newquay, where we made some good friends who owned the site. In 1977, during the Queen's Jubilee, we all went along with my brother-in-law John and his close friends Paul and Nina Todd.

Apart from the beach and coastal walks, there was plenty more on offer such as a golf course and horse riding. The latter was disastrous for us, not least of all because none of us had received any training. We all thought we were going to partake in a leisurely horse walk. This might have been the case, had the owner of the stables been available to take us, rather than a stable hand with minimum experience.

All was well and uneventful until the horses reached the beach, where obviously they had been encouraged to enjoy themselves and break out into a ferocious gallop. Disastrously, all ten of us were never expecting our horses to bolt and the resulting carnage was reminiscent of the charge of the Light Brigade, although the latter failed military action must have been a success by comparison. Several of the family members were immediately ejected from their seated positions to land ignominiously in the sand, amongst a flurry of hooves. Others, like me, had their arms locked around the bouncing necks of racing horses or clinging on for dear life to the animals' manes. The Grand National had never had so many riderless horses, and I wondered how many of us would have to be put down! As the horses eventually began to slow, riders were being ejected by saddles that were rising to meet uncoordinated descending bottoms.

At the far end of the beach, my horse came to the abrupt stop that I had been praying for but not expecting. In one movement, I was somersaulted over the head of my steed, to be slammed into the sand on my back with great force, still holding the reins. As I slowly opened my eyes, I looked up at the image of 'Mr Ed' peering down at me, wondering what he might have been thinking… 'You complete pratt' would have been a good call!

Paul, who miraculously, had remained on his horse, looked down at me with his glasses and sunhat askew and recited the strapline to a current cigarette advert of the time, which featured cowboys corralling wild horses, "Come to Marlborough Country."

I've never been on a horse since but can only look at and admire the control, skill and dexterity of Olympic equestrians, such as Laura Collett, William Fox-Pitt, or my sister-in-law Gill, although it's likely they have never ridden a horse as rogue as mine was!

After a period of recovery and therapy with a yoga instructor, the boys decided to have a round of golf. It was likely to be less eventful, wasn't it?

We agreed to have an early start so that we could all go on a shopping spree.

All was going swimmingly well until we got to the tenth hole; a par three on the links course, where Reg spotted something lying on the grass next to the teeing area, "That looks like somebody's dropped their pipe." At this point, a socially conscious individual might have placed it in their pocket and at leisure, tried to find its owner, or at least handed it into the lost property. Of course, Reg had another great idea, "Hey, this is a golf ball and tee all in one."

With that, he bent down and retrieved his own golf ball and supporting tee, replacing them with the doomed smoker's pipe. Then taking a nine-iron from the trolley, he addressed the 'ball'. Incredibly, the pick-up, swing and connection were in perfect alignment. The pipe bowl was launched with force and accuracy, some considerable distance down the fairway, much to the delight of Reg and the foreboding of the onlookers.

As we all approached the eleventh, a rather elderly, sweaty and discombobulated man came briskly walking towards us from the direction of the twelfth tee, "Oh, hello, chaps, I wonder if any of you might have spotted my new pipe on the course. I've put it down somewhere, and it was an anniversary present from my wife." While the rest of us looked down at the grass or averted our gaze, with a heavy feeling of dread or remorse, Reg politely replied...

"No, I'm afraid we haven't. Any idea where you might have lost it?"

"Unfortunately, no."

"Oh dear!" replied Reg (at the same time thinking, *Thank goodness*). "But we'll keep our eyes open and if we're fortunate enough to find it, we'll hand it in."

*Yes, in several pieces*, I thought.

"That's very kind of you," said the elderly man.

A wave, or more like a torrent of guilt washed over us all, including Reg, but again in his incorrigible manner retorted, "Well, that's gone some way towards improving his health... it was a bad habit. He'll thank us for living longer now, won't he?"

Undeniably, events were to take a turn for the worse, when we drove to Falmouth that afternoon, but in fairness, it wasn't entirely Reg's fault.

All ten of us travelled to the south coast town in Reg's utilitarian Bedford Dormobile, rather like transported convicts in a television episode of 'Heartbeat'.

Historically, it wasn't the first time Falmouth had come under ambush. Its defences had been strengthened whilst under threat from the Spanish Armada and around 1839 Falmouth was the scene of a gold robbery, when £47,000 worth of gold dust from Brazil was stolen upon its arrival at the port. Reg drove into town around noon. As he entered the busy town car park, he noticed a vacant space and couldn't believe his fortune as he carefully manoeuvred into it and switched off the engine, "Right on time, I booked this space, especially for us," he exclaimed. Everyone giggled in approval as they extricated themselves from the confined space of the vehicle.

Then to everyone's surprise, a retired-looking gentleman accompanied by a rather reticent-looking wife made a beeline for Reg and spoke in a rather terse way, "I know your sort!" he retorted.

"What holidaymakers?" replied a confused Reg.

"No, troublemakers," said the becapped, diminutive stranger.

To be fair, he had some pluck, not least of all because he was heavily outnumbered, but also because Reg was built like a proverbial brick house.

"I'm sorry?"

"You saw that I was about to take that space, and you deliberately drove in before I could."

"I had no idea you were there," replied Reg.

"Come on love, don't start an argument, I'm sure they didn't mean to," said the man's wife.

However, Falmouth's very own Victor Meldrew had other thoughts, "No, he *meant* to drive into my parking space. You people are always looking to cause trouble."

"That's not true, calm down. I had no idea you were going to take that space," said Reg.

"I'm going to call that policeman over… excuse me, officer, OFFICER!"

"That won't be necessary," implored Reg.

"We'll see about that!" said Victor.

"What seems to be the problem sir," said the archetypal policeman with his hands behind his back and rising onto the balls of his feet.

"This group of troublemakers deliberately drove into the car space I was about to park in."

"That's not true officer, I never saw him."

"All right sir, it all appears to be a misunderstanding. Look there's another space over there. Go and drive into that one, before someone else arrives."

Reluctantly, the grumpy retiree moved back to his car whilst mumbling and grumbling under his breath.

"I really didn't deliberately take his space," said Reg.

"Don't worry sir, I'm sure it wasn't intentional, but I know his type. They're like a dog with a bone. Where are you all from? Are you just here for the day?"

After a brief exchange of pleasantries, we all went off into town, quite bemused by the encounter.

Some hours later we returned in good spirits after having spent some revitalising time at the beach-front and shopping for souvenirs. As we were cramming ourselves back into the van, Reg made a discovery, "Hey, that old miserable sod's car is still parked in that space over there. I feel bad about having taken his parking space. Why don't we give him his own personal bay? Look over there. I can see a broken concrete bollard on its side. Come and help me pick it up."

No joking, it took four of us to pick the bloody thing up and struggle with it over the twenty yards or so to his vehicle, whereupon Reg instructed us to place it upright and directly behind it. I think it is known as aiding and abetting.

"There, now he's got his own parking space that no one can drive into. Unfortunately, he won't be able to get out of it either. He accused me of doing something that I wasn't guilty of, so now I feel justified in proving him right whilst providing him with a service, by way of an apology."

We promptly left the car park and drove past his blockaded vehicle with smug looks upon our faces, rather like the Down Syndrome children aboard the 'Sunshine Variety Bus' in that hilarious episode of *The Inbetweeners* at 'Thorpe Park'.

To this day, we regret not having been able to see the look on that man's face as he returned to his 'secure' parking space, but we're convinced that the words… 'I don't believe it' and 'I told you so', were mentioned and the policeman, if called back, most likely adopted a wry grin and probably secretly approved.

# Chapter Seven

Paul and Nina Todd became close friends of the family. Whilst Nina was more reserved, restrained and measured in her personality, on occasions revealing an impish nature, Paul was the antithesis. Although he could show a thoughtful, sensitive and caring side to his character, for the most part, he was, fun-loving, extremely witty and at times quite outrageous. When Reg and he got together, it was a recipe for rib-tickling moments and disastrous outcomes.

On one memorable occasion during a camping holiday in Cornwall, Paul and Reg thought it would be an amusing ruse to purchase some stink bombs from a joke shop, with the intention of releasing them in the ladies' tent. The lads and ladies always slept in separate tents, mostly because the ladies were not stupid! They always knew that the boy's accommodation would end up looking and smelling like the annual wildebeest migration had passed through it.

So, later when the girls were settled down in their billets for the night, Paul, armed with his packet of sulphurous delights, decided to perform a commando raid on the adjacent harem. The rest of the 'boys' waited in feverish anticipation as Paul quietly slipped out and unzipped the entrance to the girl's tent before placing a couple on the sealed groundsheet and stamping on them.

Suddenly, the proverbial shit hit the fan! A state of noisy disturbance and confusion ensued. Cries of the grief-stricken occupants gasping for breath, between shouts of profanity and death threats filled the night as Paul came racing back into our tent in a state of heightened jubilance and leapt backside first onto his sleeping bag. His profound excitement and sense of triumph were short-lived as the realisation of landing on the box of fragile vile phials in his back pocket swept over him, as did the concentrated vapours of their contents.

Whatever, horror-stricken moments the girls had endured in their tent, they were nothing compared to what assailed our nostrils that night. We were, if not hoisted by our own petard, briefly paralysed by the extreme shock of gas warfare. There were not enough exit points to quickly secure the life-saving qualities of fresh air. The ensuing panic forced bodies to clamber over each other in failed attempts to extract themselves from the sealed tent and groundsheet enclosure.

Hours after the turmoil had subsided, we were all back in our sleeping bags having not fully aired the tents but rather accustomed ourselves to the offending ambient odour. Still unable to sleep in the early hours, Paul decided to tell us a humorous tale of the time he came home late from a work party, worse for wear having consumed a skinful of alcohol. Nina was already asleep, so he crept into bed without disturbing her.

The following morning, he suffered a most debilitating hangover, but rather than own up to having one, he convinced Nina that he was genuinely unwell. For the rest of that day, he told us… "I was having her running around bringing, fetching and carrying me drinks, food and newspapers. To this day she has no idea that I was feigning illness and treating her like a private nurse."

He giggled mischievously to himself before a voice from the adjacent tent, cut through the following silence… "I heard that!"

Paul went pale and the rest of us laughed uproariously.

Getting back to sleep was difficult because Reg was out 'sparko' and lying flat on his back. The result of this position and having consumed vast quantities of 'Black and Velvet' (a mixture of Guinness and cider—Paul's fault) was that he continually snored like a rutting stag or a wild boar in delight at having found an enormous truffle.

"For God's sake give him a nudge," was someone's plea for silence. As I was the closest, I raised myself up and gave him a gentle rock. He grunted and snorted momentarily and then fell silent, much to the relief of the others. However, moments later he had started up again like someone fighting a grizzly with a chainsaw. I gently nudged him again, but whilst this had the desired effect, it wasn't long before the fabric of the tent was once more flapping to the sounds of a congested walrus, and it felt as if all our internal organs were reverberating.

Nearing the point of desperation, I once again rose out of my sleeping bag and gave him a hefty thump, not realising that I had made contact with his crown jewels. The response by Reg was to rear up in a jackknife position that would have impressed Tom Daley, with his hands touching the toes on his outstretched feet and eyes as wide as saucers, whilst emitting a violent rush of air as from a rotten ruptured carcass. His next utterance was…

"What the fuck was that…" strangely enough, not even who was that.

"You were snoring."

"Snoring! What punishment would I get for soiling the bed?" He didn't say 'soiling'.

From that moment, it became known as the 'Holywell Bay' treatment, and he's never let me forget it. The rest of the night was uneventful though.

# Chapter Eight

One might say my father had an unfortunate relationship with his vehicles, by which I mean he was always trying and having to repair them; mainly since he could only afford the ones that others were glad to get rid of. I have fond memories of his feet. I saw more of these than the rest of his body, as these were often sticking out from beneath his latest acquisition. He wasn't a trained mechanic, but he often came up with novel ways of overcoming unexpected challenges, like the time my brother-in-law John accidentally locked his keys into the boot of his brand-new 'Datsun Bluebird' whilst we were on holiday in Newquay. It was a wonderful car of the time and extremely reliable, even though it didn't have the technology of automatic boot release when the driver's keys were left inside.

John was beside himself as he had left the spare key at home and was about to call the breakdown services (a far more prudent course of action in retrospect) when Reg intimated that he had a better (if not highly suspect and subjective) idea. So, with skills of precision and the delicate touch of a navvy, he set about the boot-lock with a hammer and screwdriver. The resulting damage wouldn't even have been witnessed in a breaker's yard and John was subsequently faced with an unexpected bill of repair.

Even witnessing this act of well-intentioned vandalism, which should have been a warning in itself, he still made the mistake of marrying into the family—his own fault—and that wasn't the end of mishaps with this car. He later drove it to Paul and Nina's house where my brother, who was doing some weeding by the drive, unexpectedly, astonishingly and thoughtlessly, shoved the end of the hoe through the near-side wing mirror. John was dumbstruck! He had just had the car repaired. Pete did say sorry though.

Another memorable, though eminently embarrassing moment, involved my brother and I, driving with Reg in one of his old Bedford Dormobiles down the A41. I was only nine at the time, and my brother was seven.

We were driving yet again to a gardening job when my father spotted another abandoned similar van on the other side of the dual carriageway. Upon this 'fortuitous' discovery, Reg became excited and wondered if it was the source of another dynamo (alternator) as his had 'given up the ghost'. To be fair, the other vehicle looked like a wreck and appeared to have been abandoned for some considerable time. As we approached it from the north side, Reg voiced his intentions, "When we've parked up, you help me get the part off Paul and you keep a sharp lookout for any unwelcome visitors Pete"; of course, 'unwelcome' meaning police!

We had only been working on the removal of the dynamo for a few minutes, when Pete announced—with no time for us to react—that there was a man in a blue uniform wanting to speak to Dad.

Upon receipt of this 'warning', Reg poked his head out from beneath the wreck and exclaimed, "I haven't got it off yet!"

"Got what off, sir?"

Now on reflection, a casual, if not 'innocent' response of… "Oh, hello, officer, I was just examining this abandoned wreck, to see if there was any serviceable part that I might put to good use before it's towed away and dumped. Would that be permissible?" – may have possibly been more prudent and effective for a sympathetic policeman.

The officer quoted some highway or byway act, which we interpreted as, "You're nicked!"

He then proceeded to inform a rather displaced Reg, that we would all have to be questioned and possibly charged down at the local station. What alarmed Dad the most was the intention of the officers to drive him and his boys to the police station separately.

"You can't take my boys away from me, they're too young and they do as they are told."

"This appeal fell on unsympathetic ears and as they escorted us to a waiting patrol car, Reg shouted out, 'Whatever they ask, you say I don't know. I'll see you soon.'"

We were placed in the back of the patrol car and set off. For us, this action was quite alarming, and I'm sure quite unnecessary by today's standards.

Within moments, the officer turned to me and asked for my name and enquired as to where I lived. I readily gave the answers. He then turned to Pete and asked for his name to which he replied, "I don't Know."

I comforted Pete and assured him that it was fine to give them this information. Then the officer asked him where he lived, "I don't know!" was the reply to his brief.

"You're allowed to tell him that Pete."

When I reflect on this debacle, it reminds me of that hilarious line from 'Dad's Army'… "Don't tell him Pike!"

Some years later, when I was writing my first book of poetry. The title poem was based on this event:

## Official Secret

MI5
MI6
Or am I 7?

The outcome of Reg's misdemeanour was that he was to appear before the local magistrate and was advised to seek representation. Clearly, a new dynamo would have been less costly.

On the day of the court appearance, we were not brought in front of the judge, who after hearing the case, severely criticised the police for leaving the wreck by the side of the road as a means of entrapment. Indeed, two other 'offenders' had been brought to court on separate occasions to face judgement. The magistrate eventually announced that he was giving Reg a 'Conditional discharge'.

Dad heard the word 'discharge' and that was good enough for him, but his punctilious and pedantic lawyer wanted more clarification, "Your Honour, my client is either discharged or guilty. He can't be both."

"Would you prefer that I formally charge the defendant?"

Reg immediately grabbed the arm of his solicitor, "What does this mean?"

"It means they're letting you go but keeping the offence on record."

"Well, what are you waiting for? That's good enough for me. Stop winding the judge up."

"I'm not winding the judge up sir; I merely want clarification of your innocence or guilt."

"Well, here's my clarification," he whispered. "I'm very happy with that outcome, so let's wind this up instead of the judge. And then much louder: Thank you Your Honour we'll be happy to accept your findings."

That was how it all ended, fortunately for Reg, although less fortunately for the police who were instructed to remove the temptation and for the teacher accused of trying to remove the seatbelts. The latter refused to accept the judge's decision, possibly to avoid a blot on his record or even dismissal from his profession and so chose to take the case to Crown Court… where he lost.

This wasn't the only brush Reg had with the law, but many might sympathise and say he was justified in taking the action he did in this next incident:

During the early seventies, having a phone in one's home was considered an expensive luxury, in much the same way as having a mobile phone in the late eighties and quite often to cut costs, houses would agree to share a party line. To establish the privacy of the call, one had to press a button next to the receiver. If you forgot to do this, the neighbour could listen to your conversation. Although the cheaper option, it wasn't the same as having your own private line and charges were still made on each individual call made. So, we were not permitted to use the phone often.

One evening, Ruth and Reg decided to drive over to Molly's to see how she was coping. My eldest sister Angie, who was then in her mid-teens, was entrusted with the task of supervising the other four of us. She was instructed to call our grandmother's phone if there was a problem.

The evening was uneventful until Angie decided to ring one of her friends and forgot to press the party line button.

There was a 'party' going on in the neighbour's house, although it could be better described as a drug rave. To say Angie was subjected to a tirade of sexual abuse and innuendo is perhaps inadequate, given the state of shock she was reduced to. This was clearly transmitted to Reg when he received a distress call from her. How he wasn't charged with dangerous driving on his way back to us is a mystery.

What could easily be described as a journey of at least fifteen to twenty minutes on a normal day, was covered in ten minutes. Angie was still crying and being comforted by us when he burst in through the back door. His session of questioning lasted just moments before he flew back out through the door whilst Ruth prepared us all for bed.

It wasn't until the next morning that we saw him in bed nursing a badly cut and bruised hand. At that moment, neither of our parents was in a mood to share the events of the previous night, but they were clearly concerned. I say they, but it was mostly Ruth. Whomever had been on the business end of that fist, must have been rueing his previous indiscretions. We later found out that this individual's lack of good judgement had him end up in hospital.

Apparently, Reg had entered the neighbour's house on the night in question, via an open door. The excess volume of alcohol and recreational drugs that had been consumed made it virtually impossible for Reg to be heard, much less find out who had been responsible for the party line harassment. So he approached the source of the deafening sound and yanked the electrical cable from its socket. At that moment, the room fell silent and the crowd of revellers were confronted with a high-octane-fuelled and adrenalin-charged Reg, demanding to know who had been responsible for his daughter's distress and his anger-induced demeanour. The guilty party made two grave errors: He openly admitted in front of his friends, without so much as an apology or feeling of remorse in a smug and ingratiating performance and secondly, he laughed… *laughed?* He shouldn't have laughed, not to Reg's face at least, because that defiant act was the catalyst for what subsequently happened: Like a raging bull—there was no quarter given for discussion or arbitration—Reg stormed over to the individual and with one powerful right hook, rendered him senseless as the concussive force had his head literally bouncing off the wall before his limp body slid down the wall, at the base of which it came to rest, motionless.

"When he comes round, tell him to work on his social skills, particularly his phone manner," was his unsolicited advice as Reg left the building, "Oh and tell him to knock on my door and apologise to my daughter…night."

The knock at the door that came the next day, wasn't from the recipient of Dad's physical admonishment. It heralded the arrival of one P.C. John Mills, "Not the actor of course." He followed up with, after his introduction.

"May I come in?"

Although the arrival of a police officer at our front door was enough to instil a sense of panic within all of us initially, this very experienced man was adept at addressing such delicate matters and allowed us to adopt a sense of ease… to a degree.

"I'm sure you'll be aware as to why I'm here?"

"Would you like a cup of tea?" said Mum, likely praying that her kind gesture would lessen the conditional outcomes of the visit.

"That would be nice. Milk and two sugars please," said P.C. Mills, whose initials of rank would more appropriately have stood for 'political correctness', had the concept been known of in those days.

Mum could not comply quickly enough. She had no intention of being around to hear the bad news.

"Now, Mr Franklin, we've received a complaint of assault by one of your neighbours. As you know, this is quite serious, but I've come to you, rather than summon you to the station, to hear your side of the story, because the character on whom you served your own punishment is well known to us."

After questioning Reg and Angie at length, whilst scribbling down copious notes, he was able to formulate strong mitigating circumstances.

"Whilst this does not exonerate your behaviour, it certainly explains the reasons why you responded in such an aggressive and dare I say, understandable manner. I think any self-respecting and concerned parent would have done the same if they'd had possession of your physical attributes. Luckily, the individual in receipt of your justice hasn't any lasting injuries, but although he must answer charges himself, relating to drug abuse, you will I'm afraid, still have to attend court."

Astonishingly, he went on to say that he would be willing to submit a character reference to the judge. To us youngsters and Mum for that matter, we were hoping that he was referring to the plaintiff and not the defendant.

P.C. Mills was good to his word and his spoken evidence in court ultimately helped Reg to emerge from the proceedings with a clear record.

We've no idea if John Mills is still alive today, but whether he is, this reference is a testament to his kind, understanding and professional demeanour.

Party lines were not around for too long, suggesting that the phone company must have had all manner of problems with them. However, one thing is for sure, it wasn't long after this unfortunate incident that Mum and Dad had a private line installed.

The offending neighbour eventually moved out, probably to take up residence in a place of correction at Her Majesty's pleasure… and certainly ours!

# Chapter Nine

Not all our holidays were spent at campsites near the beach in Dorset or Cornwall. Enjoyable as they had been, as we got older, we kids sought more fulfilment from our vacations. In 1984, we were invited to join Paul, Nina, Angie and John on a narrowboat holiday travelling around the 'Warwickshire Ring'. Reg and Ruth were also invited. This gave John some concern and rightly so perhaps. I've always considered his relationship with Reg after the Datsun car incident, akin to that of Herbert Lom and Peter Sellers in the 'Pink Panther' film franchise.

Anyway, after a lengthy journey up the M1, we all finally arrived at the canal boatyard in Coventry to pick up the seventy-foot long, twelve-birth narrowboat and receive some preliminary training. At first glance, it did appear excessively long. The representative asked us if we had ever piloted a narrowboat, and we all said no; all of us except Reg, who said yes, of course.

Whilst reminiscing over this event, I can't help but smile and think of the studio album 'Songs for Silverman' by Ben Folds, with one line in particular from the track 'Bastard', "So why do you have to act like you know when you don't know? It's OK if you don't know everything."

As I've got older, I understand it, especially when you have children. It's an alpha male thing. I can't remember who this statement is credited to, but I too… 'remember a time when I knew more than my mobile phone'. I think the way to impress people is by admitting you don't know something and then performing some given task in an accomplished fashion, rather than the opposite. Ironically, Dad has always said to me… "Always listen to what someone has to say, even if you've heard it before." Sound advice.

We were all filled with a sense of great expectations and after paying an £80 deposit (quite a sum for the time), loading up our belongings along with enough food for a siege, we set off for our first mooring before dark.

One of the top tips given to us by the hire firm was to try not running the boat at full revs to conserve fuel and always do the required daily checks. To be fair, Reg was superb at the latter.

As the sun began to set on that first day, Reg 'gunned' the engine to full power in order to make the next lock before mooring so that we should be first through the next day. It was certainly a portent of things to come, with Reg piloting the boat at two running speeds—top and stop!

Unlike the canal and river systems in France, most locks on the system were self-operated. So, at six o'clock, the following morning, the beautiful, tranquil setting was shattered by the diesel engine being fired into life to heat the hot water on board for showers etc. Added to this pandemonium was the high-pitched whistling of the steaming kettle on the stove for tea.

Even the birds were still stretching their wings in readiness for their early morning search for insects, as the disturbed and shaken on-board crew were awoken to the sounds of the throbbing engine and the shouted instructions from the tiller by 'Captain Birdseye'.

Through sleep-filled eyes, yawns and stretching limbs came the maritime instructions, "Cast off fore and aft. Who's on tea duty?"

"No one you pillock, we're still asleep. We haven't even had breakfast yet," said John.

"No time for that," came the reply. "We've got to get through this lock and move on ahead of the other craft."

"Why, have we got to reach a time portal before it disappears forever?" said Paul.

However loud this commotion was for us, it must have been much louder for other dreaming boat-dwellers as the noise travelled across the canal and hit their vessels below the waterline.

No matter the hardships a crew of a large, tall ship encounters upon its voyage, they are nothing compared to spending a fortnight on a boat with 'Dredge' as he became known for dredging up the bottom of canals with the propeller spinning at full revolutions.

As we got underway and our over-inflated, space-hopper-sized bladders were relieved after queuing for the limited 'bathroom' facilities, normality resumed, against the backdrop of a screaming 'Lister Petter' diesel-fuelled, multi-purpose engine.

After breakfast, the weather turned inclement, and I went to the stern to see if Dad required a break. Sliding back the hatch I looked up to see an image of Reg dressed in a yellow sou'wester and oilskins looking like a skipper aboard a fishing vessel in the television series 'Deadliest Catch', braving the swells of the Bering Sea looking for king crabs,

"Do you want a break, Dad?"

"No thanks son, you get below. I'll shout when I do."

I then retraced my steps back to the front of the barge and settled down to have a game of chess with Paul.

All was going swimmingly well, despite the backdrop of the English countryside flashing by as if on video fast forward, when suddenly Paul was thrust forcibly backwards onto a storage cupboard behind him, and I was literally catapulted forwards over the flimsy table, to land unceremoniously on him. Chess pieces filled the air like exploding shrapnel, with muffled screams and sounds of loose objects and bodies impacting against the fixed interior. Then everything went quiet, except for the engine which momentarily went into reverse gear at high revs and then stopped.

After a brief moment of silence, shock and disorientation came the call, "I didn't see that coming, is everyone alright?"

"No, you complete lunatic," said a voice I couldn't quite identify. Then upside down and peering between Paul's legs, I saw a head with a cracked face-pack emerge from the bathroom, with rippled lips like the long-suffering manager of the Solana Hotel in the TV show Benidorm, played by Sherrie Hewson. *Bathroom*, let's get this straight, it was nothing more than a broom cupboard with a skimpy plastic curtain wrapped around a toilet, with a basic shower head above. When flushed, the toilet sucked down the waste with the suctional force of a jetliner's W.C. One had to stand up before flushing, or risk being vacuum-packed in the bowl!

From another bunkroom emerged one of my sisters, modelling smudged lipstick and makeup, giving her the appearance of Heath Ledger's Joker, only more sinister-looking.

Other crewmembers appeared from various stations, either in a state of undress with towel-wrapped heads or dishevelment but all displaying shocked facial expressions; some were even doused in the contents of their tea, coffee or hot chocolate cups.

When we all emerged onto the gunwale, into the drizzly, misty conditions, clutching the handrail, our predicament became apparent.

In the poor conditions, Reg had taken a short, dead-end tributary at full speed and ploughed straight into the sludgy banking at the end, with the bow clear of the waterline. Any more speed or power and the seventy-foot vessel would have been lost in woodland!

After some time and spent energy using barge poles, with Reg at his happiest thrusting the seventy-foot unguided missile into reverse and churning up centuries of silt and sediment—not to mention dead and living invertebrates that dwelt within the stagnant water—we gave up the hopeless task of refloating the stranded narrowboat.

"It's no good boys, we're going to have to get help," said Paul.

So Reg reluctantly shut down the engine whilst Paul and John went to find a phone box to ring the boatyard and the rest of us went below for a cuppa, sitting down at the fold-away table, assuming the take-off position of 'Thunderbird 2'.

About an hour later a bemused boatyard mechanic arrived at the scene, scratching his head and rubbing his chin, "It's not a 'DUKW' amphibious craft or 'Operation Overlord'."

With uncomfortable smiles and sniggers, it was hard to hide our embarrassment.

After hitching up a towrope to his smaller craft and with us providing extra leverage with the poles, the 'Coventry Queen' yielded, slowly, slurping and releasing her grip of the canal bank.

"You're lucky, there doesn't seem to be any damage to the hull. Enjoy the rest of your holiday Humphrey and Katharine," said the mechanic amusingly, looking sympathetically at Ruth and Reg, the latter still dressed in his 'John West' outfit.

The rest of the day was uneventful, possibly since someone else was piloting the boat. All remained calm when Reg was asleep or off duty.

Before we left the boatyard, one of the questions posed was how many times we should expect to empty the toilet tank. The answer given suggested only once a week. In reality, this became three times a week; an unexpected, time-consuming and costly expense, that I'm sure even the cross-channel ferries didn't incur or require. Even fresh water for showers and consumption had to be topped up every other day!

Ironically, I have to say, I cannot over-emphasise or extol the virtues or experience of a canal boat holiday. Not least of all for its soothing, calming and relaxing qualities, with life passing you by at four miles an hour. It's one of the fastest ways to slow down, along hundreds or even thousands of miles of waterways, packed with wildlife.

As well as the feeling of liberation and spending priceless, quality time with family and friends, there are limitless ways of exercising, such as opening and closing locks, roping up or cycling along the towpath. There's plenty of time for relaxation in the evenings and wonderful historic places to visit. In addition, we stopped at just about every pub with a dartboard and played some wonderful games, involving many locals who marvelled at Reg's skills; both throwing and mathematical calculations, including all the related permutations.

The greatest benefit in my opinion is the absence of a television set, allowing for the resurgence of group or board games or more importantly, constructive, invaluable debate.

With our family and friends, it was a laugh a minute, even when Peter and Paul ended up crashing through a bunkroom door after a mock wrestling match. This alone may have cost us our deposit, had it not been for the skills of my brother who was a confident and accomplished carpenter.

We were all filled with a sense of fulfilment, rest, happiness and satisfaction, if not a little anticlimax, when we arrived back at the boatyard; not least of all for getting the narrowboat back on time and more importantly, in one piece! In addition, we had decided to spend our deposit on an end-of-holiday restaurant meal that night.

As we unloaded our possessions into the cars and briefly cleaned the interior before the inspection, John, Paul and Reg went to the boatyard office to sign in and retrieve the deposit.

After what seemed an interminable length of time, all three returned to the waiting group, who by this time had loaded the cars and attended to the interior and exterior cleaning of the boat. All had serious expressions on their faces.

"What's the matter with you lot?" said Ruth as they approached.

"It's not good," said Paul.

"We've lost our deposit!" said John.

"What?!!" we all replied in unison.

Apparently, the exchange of dialogue with the boat company was as follows, "Welcome back, Mr Franklin, I'm afraid I have some bad news regarding your deposit. We are unable to refund it."

"Why on earth not? The boat is undamaged."

"Yes, that's fine, but we've had a complaint from a number of residents in Birmingham."

"*Birmingham?* But we never stopped at Birmingham."

"Precisely, you didn't, but you should have."

"Should have, why? We didn't want to."

"Understood, but you should have stopped and picked up a professional pilot, who would have navigated your boat through the very shallow draft at that junction. Unfortunately, you carried on through the pilot zone at full speed, creating a damaging wake which buffeted and bounced the smaller houseboats against the banks of the moorings, creating a great deal of internal damage. Crockery and other unsecured items were smashed."

"But they came out and waved at us," said Reg.

"Yes, with their fists. They were trying to slow you down. We also had complaints from house residents whose gardens back onto the canal, to say you were scrumping their apples from the boat as you went by."

"Yes, but the fruit was overhanging the fences on our side of the canal. It made some nice pies."

"Yes, I'm sure Mr Franklin but the trees were planted in their gardens, hence their fruit."

"The bill for the damage is far more than your deposit and will be covered by our insurance company."

"Well, please pass on our sincerest apologies," said John… and Paul… and Reg in succession.

There was no celebratory meal that evening, just a long tiresome journey back, with enough time for quiet reflection and remorse.

# Chapter Ten

Our time spent on the Warwickshire Ring canal boating gave us all a keen interest and involvement in this kind of leisure holiday, so it was with great excitement that we all signed up for a three-week break on the Canal Du Midi in France, along with Paul's suggestion. It took some planning and preparation, taking three cars, twelve people—including Barbara's boyfriend Dave, plus a friend of Pete's—and a large, hired trailer, but being the late eighties and out of season, the entire expenditure for the holiday worked out at only one hundred pounds per person. On top of this, most of us could drive, which meant there would be minimal delays in covering the journey.

One exciting element of the journey involved crossing the Channel on the hovercraft, which saved us much time as it only took twenty minutes. It's hard to see why this form of transport went out of business.

We stopped at a hotel a few hours after the crossing and immediately immersed ourselves in the French culture. Paul's mother was French, so he had a reasonable command of the language and the rest of us put our limited secondary school knowledge to the test.

I've always believed that tourists or immigrants should try and speak the language of the country they visit. People who speak three languages are tri-lingual, people who speak two are bi-lingual and those who speak one are British! Somehow, speaking louder and slower to foreigners in English just reinforces the fact that you are just an arrogant, if not ignorant, nationalistic person.

With the possible exception of some Parisians that I've encountered, an overwhelming number of French people will only be too happy to help you out because they can, if you at least make an effort to speak their language. If they suspect you are struggling, quite often they will say in their romantic, lilting accent, "Tu preferes l'anglais?"

Construction on the Canal du Midi began in 1667 and was completed in 1681. It is 240 kilometres long and considered to be one of the greatest construction works of the seventeenth century. Its starting point is in Toulouse, and its endpoint is Etang de Thau on the Mediterranean. It is a magnificent feat of engineering and blends in beautifully with its surrounding landscape. It is bordered by thousands of plane trees which not only look enchanting but effectively reinforce the erosional effects on the banks.

Sadly, many have been cut down due to the spread of a deadly canker stain, but newly planted saplings will gradually recreate the former beauty of their predecessors. The canal passes through a large area of wine-producing regions and is simply spellbinding during the grape harvest. It remains one of the top three holiday destinations I have had the pleasure to visit in my life! This particular visit was before my teaching career and sadly for over twenty-five years, it was impossible for me to return in the autumn. I would have genuinely given back eight weeks of school holidays, spent travelling at the most popular and expensive times, to have returned for just ten days during September.

It is very different from our canal network system for several reasons: Firstly, it's much wider and has lock operators, which you are expected to tip. Secondly, there are greater choices for mooring a wider birth launch and thirdly, the locks shut down between 12:00 and 1400 hours for lunch. What's more, is that most will sell fresh bread and other produce to eat during this time. Very civilised indeed.

Each morning, we cycled to the next lock or boulangerie to pick up our daily 'pain' which of course was anything but, in terms of the English spelling, unlike our tortuous cycle seats! Our intake of bread and wine was well beyond the partaking of any religious ceremonial worshipping. We all put at least half a stone on during this break!

We were only a few days into our remote idyllic waterway retreat when Reg decided to bring our vessel to the bank for mooring at lunchtime. This normally perfunctory exercise suddenly brought back nightmares of our narrowboat calamity, as the biggest grinding noise since the barman on board the Titanic asked for more ice, rent the air. John was first to ask, "What's Captain Pugwash done this time?"

As he looked down from his sunbathing position upon Paul who was holding the front mooring rope, "I don't know, but it sounds very expensive!" came the reply.

To be honest, the long ominous tear in our hull was not caused by reckless piloting but by a submerged, hidden piece of steel gantry, which once supported a wooden raft.

The lunch break was unavoidably lengthened as we waited for assistance to arrive. When it eventually did, a very kind and understanding shipwright made an effective patch from fibreglass and assured us that his report would record that it wasn't our fault… luckily!

The idea behind the cooking and cleaning rota was Paul's and quite inspired. It involved the twelve of us organising ourselves into six pairs, with any pair on a given day doing the three meals, all the cleaning, making drinks and generally carrying out any 'bring me, fetch me, carry me' waitering required. Yes, this meant working hard for one day, but then having five days off.

Any pair missing duties on an ad hoc day out would simply work a shift towards the end of the holiday. This meant that each pair would only work for two days in the entire three-week holiday. The chores were not that much of a drag either. There was still time in the day to relax and the evening meals were fantastic as a level of competition was factored in.

On one enjoyable but uneventful day, we moored up outside a small parochial village with the intention of walking in to find a restaurant. After a lengthy 'musical-bathrooms' scenario, we all set off to find a suitable hostelry.

As I stepped onto the narrow, insecure gangplank, I lost my footing and subsequently, my leg scudded ominously down the side of it. As is the case when one knows that they have sustained a significant injury, there was a brief moment of, "Oh dear, this is going to hurt," before the expected pain inevitably arrives. And arrive it did, as the skin on my shin was stripped away to the bone!

Blood literally pumped from an exposed blood vessel as I cursed the bad timing of my situation… as if there was a fortuitous moment for any injury!

Calling to the others for assistance, I was carried back into the boat in order to sit down and elevate my legs.

I apologised for the inconvenience and suggested that we bandage the wound and resume the walk into the village. The others were having none of it and Paul went to call a doctor.

It was some time before he arrived but when he did, he wasted no time in addressing the problem. He applied a yellow-orangeish antiseptic by brush, which was likely to be Povidone-iodine and then threaded a large-looking needle. I was half expecting him to administer a pain-relieving injection which never came, but the ensuing agony did as he set about stitching up my torn limb without the benefit of an anaesthetic. The air was as blue as the cheese we'd bought that lunchtime.

Nina told me to stop making a fuss and behaving like a wailing child as the doctor sewed me up as if preparing a Sunday joint. In a phrase most likely to come from the vocabulary of Hercule Poirot, he made a reference to the English culinary tradition, "It eez like preparation of the rost beef n'est pas?"

Looking around at the contorted expressions of my family, it was nothing like it. My request for a stick was responded to with a suggestion that it might assist my walking, "No, I want to hit this French comedian!"

We didn't go out that night as the money for food went towards the settlement of the medical intervention. I still have the scar and the memory of that evening and having seen the film 'Rambo' where Sylvester Stallone administers similar first aid to himself in the woods, I am convinced that he would have totally wussed it in real life! Even Nina admitted that it looked painful but tried to make light of it.

In truth, after witnessing the opening scenes to 'Saving Private Ryan', my injury pales into insignificance, though it did make mine and everyone else's eyes water; including the doctor who obviously thought it was amusing… bastard!

A few days later, we moored up at another spot and went to search for a restaurant. We couldn't find one but were directed to a nearby farmhouse where as informed, a woman often welcomed guests for supper.

All twelve of us were invited into her home for an impromptu meal. The interior was that of a classic farmhouse: large inglenook fireplace, an enormous, distressed oak table with a marvellous patina and suspended pans on an iron rack. The floor comprised large flagstones and was covered in a partially threadbare carpet. The woman and her two sons were very hospitable and provided bottles of wine as we sat down and surveyed the room.

The French somehow have a greater sense of respect for their food. Firstly, it is always a family affair, and there is always a stream of individual dishes that arrive at the table, rather than a competition to see who can get the most on their plate, as I have often seen at 'Toby Carveries'.

To say we had a wonderful evening with fine fare doesn't do the evening justice. Then came the bill! Paul let out a sigh and said that it couldn't be right.

All at once the lady became agitated and extremely uncomfortable.

"Il est a prix eleve—too expensive m'sieur?"

"Non, non, Madame ce n'est pas assez—it's not enough!"

The total for twelve people having eaten and drunk her out of house and home was approximately seventy-five pounds.

Paul said that we should be careful not to upset the local economy and suggested we give her one hundred pounds. In addition, we availed ourselves of as many gifts and produce as she had on show. We thanked her and her sons profusely and virtually staggered out under the weight of purchased goods and the effects of too much alcohol. No subsequent meal came as close to the feast we shared that night.

On our journey, we were invited to sample the excellent victuals of a bed-and-breakfast accommodation where, for the first time ever I was introduced to 'Munster' cheese. At the end of our meal, the proprietor brought forward the cheese from his outside window shelf, wrapped in what looked like an old oily rag.

If you've never sampled it, I can only say that Reg said it smelt like… "A skunk's foreskin!" Not that I have had the 'pleasure' of investigating the nether regions of either a skunk or polecat, but I would hazard a guess that the aroma is quite similar and that's why he kept it on the outside windowsill. Surprisingly and ironically, as the house owner explained, the taste of this cheese from the Vosges is nothing like the smell which heralds its arrival. It has a very mild and subtle taste.

Of course, Reg bought some and the French owner placed it in a plastic container for him to bring back to the boat. It stank the whole place out for the rest of the holiday.

I occasionally buy some when Gwynneth is away and keep it in the fridge within a leaded box, in much the same way as Superman stores his Kryptonite!

Undoubtedly, one of the greatest pleasures of any holiday such as a boating trip, is the absence of a television, which obviously lends itself to the rare opportunity of conversing with one's family or playing games. During one such occasion when Dad wasn't at the tiller end, 'stronging it' to the next destination, I had a lengthy conversation with him. The others thanked me for this break, but that wasn't my intention. I asked him what he would call his mansion house, should he one day come by enough money to afford it, "Oh, that's easy son, I'd call it 'Sod Hall' or 'Bugger Hall' because that's all I've ever had!"

The journey back home was long and uneventful, except for the fact that we always, *always* get stopped by the customs officers when arriving back off the ferry.

"Pull over sir, where have you been? Did you have a nice holiday?"

"Yes," said Reg, "right up to the point where we have to endure yet another search."

Embarrassingly, they emptied out all the suitcases and spread the three-week-old underpants and knickers on the ground, on top of the smelly towels they were wrapped in. Ironically, they found and never said a word about the wine and alcohol that we so painstakingly had hidden amongst our belongings.

It makes one wonder how on earth so many illegal immigrants find their way into our country, but I fear many must have taken advantage of the distractions our searches have provided.

# Chapter Eleven

As a head teacher, I once used Reg's confidence trickster skills to my advantage at Donnington Middle School Oxfordshire, but before I explain how I should put the event into context.

At this time, I was working away from home during the week and travelling back for the weekend.

One Sunday evening, whilst returning to my digs in Eynsham from West Yorkshire, I became aware that I had not packed any underwear. I called Gwynneth to request that she send me a few pairs down in a jiffy bag. This she did, addressing the package to 'the head teacher, Donnington School…' without the addition of 'Private and Personal'.

You're probably ahead of me. The package didn't come to me personally but was opened by a rather surprised secretary; one of three to be precise, with whom she insensitively shared the contents. The next thing I know is that Jane, in an act of discreditable and wanton abandonment, if not betrayal, photocopied my underwear and pinned multiple duplicates on the staffroom walls!

It's impossible to relate to the reader, the depth of my embarrassment; not merely because of this invasion of my most intimate apparel, but because they weren't exactly 'NEXT' hipsters.

Oh no, Gwynneth had managed to pick out and send, remnants of a battle-worn wardrobe that should have been burnt and buried years before. Instead, I was faced at every turn with this humiliating view of grandpop's trench-warfare Y-fronts!

And that wasn't the only embarrassing moment that Jane had instigated:

Just before the end of term, I was giving out the usual achievement awards to pupils. Jane had given me a lengthy list of pupil names, that I sometimes struggled with, because of their pronunciation. Notwithstanding, I duly concentrated and was thankful when I got to the last name, which I read out with the same conviction as those preceding it.

"And finally, last but not least Huge Jarce!"

As soon as I had uttered it, I realised that Jane had set me up… again! The whole school burst into raucous laughter, and she was almost falling off her seat with mirth. I started laughing too, for the children had to see that I was human after all and besides, it *was* funny, and there was nothing more that I could do… at this point!

Enter Reg, stage right, some months later into the reception area of Donnington Middle School as an angry and irate grandparent with an axe to grind.

He couldn't gain entrance into the building because of the security door I'd fitted, but he was nonetheless, in an aggressive mood. Swearing and cursing at the office staff, he insisted on seeing me, "I don't care if he is busy, get that twat of a head teacher out here now!"

Jane came to the hall where I was teaching and asked if I could come to calm this irate visitor down. I told her that I was busy and that she'd have to deal with it. When she got back to the entrance hall, the visitor was not in the slightest, put off by her message. Again, he became very irritated, "Look I'm not leaving here without a meeting with that complete idiot of a head. He's done nothing to help my grandchild."

Despite, her protestations he was insistent and continued to rant.

Back came Jane to say that the situation was deteriorating, but I was not going to let an angry parent override our appointment protocol. I sent her back and carried on teaching.

Back at the office, other staff were having no success in assuaging this man's anger. One of my secretaries said she would have no choice but to call the police. This threat did nothing to deter him, if anything, it made the situation worse. He threatened to kick down the door and go looking if they didn't bring me to him.

Once again Jane came to the hall; she could see that I was cross, but arrived in a state of discombobulation and visibly shaken, "Alright," I said, comforting her… "Get me some cover, and I'll return with you this time."

She quickly sourced a member of staff, and we then went back to the office together.

To her horror, I went to open the security door, "No, leave it shut, and I'll call the police."

"Don't worry I'll soon deal with this." And opened the door, "Hi, Dad, are you being a nuisance again?"

"Afraid so, son. Are you well?"

We embraced each other as the realization of the incident became apparent on the faces of the on-looking staff.

"You bastard!" Jane cried, looking at me and then turning to Dad repeating her profanity, "Mr Bastard to you, show some respect for my father. Remember my pants and Hugh?"

It was great to see Mum and Dad (Mum had waited in the car.) I had invited them primarily, to see my school for the first time. I know they were proud of my achievements. The time spent with them after a tour of the school afforded the time to reminisce. We spoke about the times as young lads and how Pete and I helped Reg with his gardening jobs.

At weekends, we would laugh along with Dad as we drove in his old Bedford Dormobile to the various gardening jobs in Edgware and Chorleywood.

I remember vividly, how hard Reg worked; in fact, how we all did to help make ends meet.

Sweat used to pour off his brow and the house-owners would always get sixty-seconds worth of minute run from him.

Some used to exploit him terribly and drive down the hourly rate. At one lawn-laying job, he was paid five shillings an hour, or twenty-five pence in today's money.

One employer even asked him, if he was the type who took two hours to complete a job when one would do!

I got so cross one weekend that I said to my father, "One day, I'm going to pull this family out of the gutter!"

It was an inappropriate use of the hyperbole, but nevertheless, a remark borne out of a genuine feeling of despondency.

When Dad found alternative employment, he gave me his gardening jobs. The first thing I did was increase the hourly rate by 100%. I had lost them all within a month and cared not a jot. Then I set about establishing my own business and eventually obtaining a degree and making my way into teaching.

You would be amazed at the change in people's stuffy, middle-class condescending attitude when they find out you're a teacher, let alone a head teacher.

Dad for many years had worked nights; it paid better money, and he had five kids and a wife to support.

When he came home from his night shift, he would often tell us stories about the high jinks he'd become involved in at the 'Sun Printers', such as passing a short length of hose under toilet doors. The anxious occupants would squirm from side to side, in an effort to dodge the expected torrent of water they thought was coming and then Dad would throw a bucket of water over the top instead!

On another occasion, he passed a large industrial-sized padlock through the buttonhole of someone's new coat and locked it. When the owner came to put it on, the weight of it nearly pulled him over. He had to carry it home with the padlock still attached!

He once stopped someone from pinching his sweets without asking, by placing foil-wrapped laxatives in the bag!

He had a close black friend in the print and one night whilst they were cleaning their hands Dad said flippantly, "You're going to have to scrub your hands harder than that, to get them like mine!"

His friend came back with a withering, humorous reply, "And you're going to have to work a lot harder to get yours like mine!"

They had a great 'Love Thy Neighbour' relationship; all right for the time perhaps but certainly politically incorrect and unacceptable today!

My father is quite literally colour-blind but his condition could just as easily be related to racial and cultural issues. He would often say to us, "Forget racism, I have an instant dislike of the type of person who sits on their lazy backside and expects the Government to look after them. They come in all sorts of shapes and sizes. Foreigners are more willing to do the jobs that they're not prepared to do!"

Without a doubt, on the subjects of racism and inequality, activists are pushing against an open door.

When I asked Dad if those people he played tricks on ever got their own back on him, he said they tried very hard, but he was always on 'high alert'.

It's true that Reg's humour has been inherited by his children, such as the time when Pete and I, along with our brother-in-law John, went to visit an old WW2 airfield in Lincolnshire.

East Kirkby is home to the largest Bomber Command Museum in the country and the only place to see a Lancaster bomber other than the Battle of Britain Memorial Flight one, being refurbished for flight. For a cost, one can taxi in this aircraft, until it becomes flightworthy.

It's possible to stand yards away from it as it goes through its warm-up protocol.

Anyway, before we witnessed this spectacle and as we walked around the airfield, John informed me that Pete had disappeared off to the toilet block. That was my cue to test out one of Reg's manoeuvres on my sibling. And make no mistake, he would have cherished the same opportunity!

Age is no determinant for practical jokes. So off I strode to the block, where in a line of cubicles, I spotted a locked door. I proceeded to fill up the coffee cup I had been drinking from with water and in one deft movement, hurled the contents over the door where my brother had taken up residence... or so I thought!

No sounds were issued from within, so thinking that I had missed, I hastily followed this up with another attack and then a third when still, no reaction was forthcoming. Then, I heard the system flush and the door opened, whereupon a soaked, diminutive, balding fellow emerged, with whatever hair he had left in disarray, stride past me, with a determined look on his face to reach the exit! I was horrified and apologised profusely as I tried to stop him to explain my prank, whilst he was having none of it and possibly wishing he was bigger.

My attempts to assuage this unfortunate man's indignation, fell on deaf ears as he exited the block. I called out to Pete, who responded from the furthest cubicle after flushing his own toilet.

"I was half expecting you to come up with some trick whilst I was in there. You missed your chance."

# Chapter Twelve

Whilst growing up all five children had their own designated weekly tasks to do, to help around the house. One of mine was to clean *every* pair of footwear over the weekend. Each one of us would put all our shoes, wellies and sportswear into a large egg box (the type that would hold twenty-four trays) and Dad would place it outside in the garden for me, so as not to create a mess indoors.

Mum would *always* tell us how expensive shoes were and how we should look after them. If they were new, they had to be softened or 'worn in' before going out in them. If we came indoors with our shoes on, we'd be told off and… 'God help you' if you damaged them at school or whilst playing out.

In a published book of poetry, I wrote in later years as an adult, one of the titles refers to this obsession Mum had, about looking after shoes to save money:

## Goody Two Shoes

I've got a new pair of shoes
So, I've got to wear them in
Before I can wear them out
But Mum says I must never wear them in (doors)

And I definitely mustn't wear them out
I wish I'd bought a pair of plimsolls now

Anyway, we were on half-term holiday this particular week, so I decided to clean the shoes on a Friday, as I would of course be helping Dad over the weekend.

When I went out into the garden to start, I couldn't find the shoes; they simply weren't there.

So, I came back in and asked Dad where he'd put them.

"In the usual place, son—by the bin. You can't miss them."

"They're not there!"

After a few heated exchanges, it became apparent to Dad that indeed, they were not there. What became even more apparent, was the fact that the bin-men came on a Friday!

I have a lasting image of Dad running out of the house in stockinged feet, chasing after the bin-lorry wielding an 'adze'.

He returned four hours later in a terrible state; out of breath and triumphantly holding up one, yes one high-heeled shoe. I thought he was going to pass out through lack of oxygen.

However, in bringing back only one shoe, he had made two fundamental errors; firstly, no one could wear it without the other and secondly, it only served to give Mum a weapon with which she could hit him… and she did!

When news got out about this unfortunate event, a friend of my mother's—an ardent church-goer—approached her vicar for some help. He advised us all to attend church that Sunday, and he would ask for a collection. We all attended (some more reluctant than others) in 'flip-flops'.

After the collection, the vicar said the church would keep half of it and gave Mum the rest. The residual amount, although gratefully received, would only be enough to buy half of our footwear, so three of us attended school for a week in flip-flops. I was at secondary school!

Dad was thankful, believe me, but a little disgruntled about this fifty-fifty arrangement at his time of need (a need to appease Mum) and I recall him saying to the vicar, "At least I didn't have to pay to get out of church this time!"

Back came the vicar's riposte, "I'm surprised you can remember!"

# Chapter Thirteen

I remember one morning being called into Mum and Dad's bedroom, in a tone that suggested urgency and direct passage, with no opportunity to 'pass go and collect two hundred pounds'. Something had definitely stirred Reg and the letter he was holding didn't look like a bill. He intimated that it was from the council with complaints from residents at a nearby block of flats, relating to disturbances, vandalism and disrespect, for all of which I was being held responsible!

As he read out the indictment, I was appalled at the accusations. To be fair, Reg said if these were true and I owned up, he would look favourably upon my honesty. I should still be punished no less. I emphatically denied the charges and despite a very lengthy interrogation, found it hard to convince Dad of my innocence. After what seemed an intolerable length of time and to his credit, Dad said that he would ask one more time and trust my final answer, but God help me if I was found out to be lying!

Eventually, after a passionate plea of not guilty and suspecting that I was telling the truth, he suggested that I be taken to the aforementioned flats for an 'identity parade'. To his consternation, this of course unsettled me because I was worried that the elderly residents would only be too pleased to have *any* spotty teenager brought back to them, to face the consequences of their displeasure. In essence, I underestimated their ability and desire to bring the right culprit to justice and Dad was adamant that they would not convict the wrong lad anyway.

So, the very next day, off we went to the residential flats to carry out our own—by which I mean Reg's—investigations and identity parade.

Our first port of call was the leader of the resident's association who had been mentioned in the letter of complaint. He took us to see the lady who had identified the perpetrator. I tried to swallow, but my mouth was too dry. Why on earth I felt trepidatious is beyond me.

Within moments of being presented to her, this lovely old lady at once said that it wasn't me that she had confronted. In an instant, I felt relieved and almost wanted to hug her. To be honest, I probably would have, had it not been for the sight of her stubble.

"Right then, thank you for your help and now we must carry out further enquiries," said Reg.

"I should start at the secondary school," said the lady, "He was definitely the same age as your son, and I got a good look at him. I'll give you a description."

Armed with this information and very much reassured that his son wasn't a reprehensible delinquent (my words, not his) Reg, to his credit and loss, took a day off work and went to the local secondary school (not the one I went to) to see the head teacher. He requested that he should like to carry out an identity parade; he was obsessed with this notion, probably because he had been in one or two himself. Strangely Reg thought this was wholly reasonable, not so the head teacher who politely declined, in favour of carrying out an investigation of her own using the description Reg gave her.

Reg was invited back at his earliest convenience—which had to be lunchtime—to be appraised of her findings.

When he returned, the head had made progress, to the extent of knowing who the individual was responsible for the deformation of my character.

Reg was eager for her to give him a name, but understandably, she politely refused due to child protection. However, Reg was insistent because he wanted to go to the police and council, to clear my name. He assured her that he wouldn't approach the boy directly. In the end, convinced of this promise, she gave him the name and said she would follow it up.

"Don't bother," said Reg. It's my next-door neighbour's son; the little sod! I'll talk to his dad.

Thanking the head for her assistance, Reg left and waited for the father of this individual to return from work. Then, like a trap-door spider, he accosted him as he alighted from his vehicle and made him an offer that he couldn't refuse. Being a man of few words, Reg's suggestion was that the father could take his son to the authorities himself or failing that, he would... "Drag the boy kicking and screaming to the police, by his hair," whilst metering out his own form of punishment on them both! "Your choice!" Correctly imagining the former option to be preferable, he took Reg up on the less painful choice the next day.

That night, we all witnessed the carnage that broke out through the wall of our semi-detached.

Whatever hiding the boy received would have been otherwise moderate by comparison to Dad's form of justice!

Nevertheless, Reg demanded that my name be struck from the records and insisted that the council write a letter of apology and exoneration to me! This they duly did. I've always been immensely grateful for the vindication and the way he defended my honour. It would have always been so, as I would not have liked to confront him, should I have been stupid enough to have been guilty.

For all his faults, Reg possessed a sense of honour, community spirit and self-respect. In truth, he would defend and support anyone in need and would often end up out of pocket.

I remember him losing a considerable amount of money for the time by helping a crying woman in a supermarket, who had allegedly *lost* her purse due to theft. Reg subsequently paid for all the victim's shopping, only to find out later that she had conned another good Samaritan out of a substantial sum, with the same sob story.

Once, the whole family went to support my older sisters who were performing in an event at the village 'Girl Guides' hut. During the show, everyone was shocked into silence as a brick came through one of the panes of glass.

Reg was 'out of the blocks' like an Olympian and disappeared out of the front door. He was gone for what seemed like an age, at least thirty minutes, but eventually came back, once again bursting through the doors and drenched in sweat. This time accompanied by a reluctant teenager, looking very much the worst for wear, who Reg, literally dragged to the stage in front of a subdued and surprised audience, "This little low-life was responsible for throwing that brick. I've managed to persuade him (*persuade him*) to come back and apologise for the disruption and damage. His friend got away, but I've got his name." Of course, he did, by battering the information out of him.

Reg had indeed chased the offender to the point of exhaustion, whereupon capturing him, he had administered his own form of justice and sentencing before dragging him back to face the music. Ironically, at that point, they were closer to the local police station than the guides' hut, and I'm guessing that 'toe-rag' would have preferred to have been taken to the former.

This kind of social safeguarding or 'upstanding citizenship' was typical of my father's age, and I take some comfort from news reports today, that there seems to be a growing number of the public who are willing to tackle this type of vandalism, robbery or attack and not just feisty old ladies with flying handbags. Yes, there is a risk to life and limb but people would feel safer going out and fewer families suffering terrible bereavement, if more of the public were willing to come to a victim's aid in numbers, if required.

One also cannot fail to notice how many more people roar around in their vehicles, primarily at school drop-off or pick-up times, but generally with a heightened degree of selfishness and disregard for other road users. Many often show an unwillingness or inability to wait or reverse their cars, even when the situation dictates so. This problem has obviously grown with the burgeoning population, the increased number of cars per family and of course as I've got older and less tolerant. Road rage was never a term used when I was a child, though I do recall isolated incidences.

When I had just entered my teens, my Uncle Harry died. Our son is named after him and a relative in Gwynneth's family. It always irritates me, when ignorant people presume he was named after Harry Potter, a character whose adventures were becoming popular after his birth. I fail to understand how some parents entertain the idea of naming their children after actors, make-believe characters or footballers, with whom they have no attachment, equations, aircraft, weather, or places where they were conceived, such as 'Brent Cross' or 'Penistone'.

Equally bemusing is when they name their offspring after a race of people, astronomical objects or even food! As a teacher, I've come across them all, even the 'cut-and-shut' of two names the parents couldn't decide upon. Don't they know these children have to grow up and find their way in the world? It's going to be hard for someone called 'Silverskin Pickles', 'Roma Star-Bright' or 'Orange-Petal Bath Bomb', to introduce themselves at a job interview, or when presenting at a United Nations Climate Change Conference!

Back to the point, Uncle Harry was the husband of Reg's sister 'Midge' or Marion. I loved them both for their kindness and warmth. I recall with equal amounts of gratitude and regret, the time my Uncle Harry presented me with his collection of 'Victor' comics. He had meticulously stored every copy over ten years from 1960 to 1970; lovingly wrapped in brown paper and string. They would have been worth a small fortune today.

I loved reading the stories relating to 'The Tough of the Track'—whose preferred, carbohydrate-enriched diet of fish and chips before every race, inspired me to skip school meals in favour of them—and of course 'Braddock of the Bombers' (V.C. and Bar). Unfortunately, I didn't quite understand the notion of posterity and to my utter shame, these comics found themselves distributed all over the house until Ruth got so fed up that she gave them to a jumble sale, along with my beloved 'Fantastic' collection. I still think of his generosity and bathe in my stupidity.

Harry's funeral was attended by many and the vehicle cortege was very long indeed. Reg and the rest of us ended up right at the back of this queue in his Bedford Dormobile. So, you can imagine that he wasn't very pleased when some impatient driver started to toot his horn behind him. Up ahead, people were showing respect for the deceased by removing hats and bowing their heads, whilst this intolerant and disgruntled individual, showed little consideration for the bereaved.

The first toot just annoyed Reg, who reacted by simply voicing his contempt. The second one prompted him to stop his van, slide back his driver's door and confront the source of his displeasure. Opening the door of the other vehicle he simply said, "Are we in a hurry, this is a funeral. Would you like to join my sister's husband in the hearse?"

With that, he pulled the driver out of his car and punched him backwards, across the bonnet.

Onlookers applauded as Reg got back into his van and brought up the rear of the convoy once again.

"Sorry about that, Duc," apologising nonchalantly to Ruth.

"You've ripped the shoulder of your jacket!"

"Harry won't mind. Shall I go back and ask that bloke to pay for it?"

Dad was always one for handing out his own kind of principled punishments; something I believe was handed down to him by his war-time serving brothers. We never crossed him, that's for sure, though I for one was always taking him to the limit of his patience, like the time he came indoors and the music centre was too loud, "Oi, turn that doings down!"

In a patronizing tone, that would be very much annoying if any pretentious child had the temerity to try it out on me, I would slowly sound out v.o.l.u.m.e.

Having already riled him to the point of frustrated incandescence, he would struggle to get his next words out, "The doings are too loud!"

"The doings? You mean the s.p.e.a.k.e.rs?" This was delivered in much the same tone as when talking to a deaf care home resident.

When the barrage of expletives or obscenities came, that was my cue to carry out the request, before he carried out the threat!

My brother would often say… "I wish you wouldn't do that!" I soon learnt not to but it was a trait picked up through behavioural observations.

# Chapter Fourteen

Reg would work hard to make his garden look at least well maintained if not impressive, so understandably, he would instantly take exception to anyone violating his horticultural endeavours.

I recall the time when he witnessed a football come flying into our front garden, closely followed by two youths trampling across his borders to retrieve it, then exiting whilst leaving the gate open, all without the courtesy of seeking permission. This wanton or thoughtless vandalism, showing the same level of disregard that the golf-club-wielding 'Inbetweeners' had for a property owner's daffodils, had the same response from a horrified Reg.

Leaping out of the front door and in hot pursuit, he tore a strip off the boys leaving them slightly traumatised, though arguably better equipped educationally, to follow a more acceptable protocol in the future.

Reg came back in and resumed a period of relaxation in his armchair, until again he was disturbed by an ominous, almighty and thunderous hammering on the front door. Pete and I briefly made uncomfortable eye contact before following him out.

As Reg opened the door, he was confronted by an enraged father with two smug-looking (that was a mistake) boys at his side, demanding to know why Reg had threatened them. In fairness, his initial hostile demeanour changed somewhat as he panned up towards the full extent of Reg's imposing frame. The boys became less self-satisfied as Reg bellowed, "What do you want? One knock at the door would have been enough for me to hear."

The man was of stocky build, with a balding head. The latter had not escaped Reg's attention, and I wondered how long it would be before he managed to refer to it within the dialogue.

"Why don't you pick on someone your own size," the father said.

"I can't see anyone my size, but I'm willing to teach both you and your sons some manners."

As the man thought discretion and retreat were the better part of valour, he backed out of the gate and with enough distance between him and Reg, yelled out, "I'll get the authorities on to you. You've bitten off more than you can chew."

"Looking at your head, it looks like you've bitten off more than you can chew, Baldy!"

Yep, there it was, right on cue. As the flustered individual chuntered on and disappeared from view, Reg looked at us and said, "Honestly, a bit of politeness never hurt anyone." I think the irony was lost on him.

Reg was in the garden on another occasion, working away when Ruth came out to remind him that our cousins were due to arrive, and she wanted him to show his face, even though she knew he was reluctant to do so.

Sometime after their arrival, Reg had still not made contact, so Ruth sent me out to *remind* him. I came back into the living room and informed her of his coming.

A short while later Reg, in his overalls and wellingtons entered the lounge and to the utter astonishment and disbelief of everyone present, performed a three-hundred-and-sixty-degree pirouette, whilst simultaneously rending the air with a six-second, variable-toned fart.

I would have been impressed with a ballerina executing that manoeuvre, obviously without the sound effects, but for Reg in all his irreverential splendour, achieving a rapid whirl of his substantial frame with one leg held out horizontally, whilst dressed in constricting overalls and 'Daisy Roots' was spectacular if not majestic. He then bowed, as if wishing to encourage the 'audience' to acknowledge his performance and departed.

The shocked and dumbfounded visitors were stunned into silence, whilst Ruth and I roared with uncontrollable laughter. They left shortly afterwards.

"Have they gone yet?" said Reg later returning to the room.

"Oh yes," said Ruth, "That ruse most definitely worked. They were most impressed, You pleb!"

Many years later, I wrote two published poems as a tribute to Reg and invited him to read them from the anthology 'Most Secret':

# Without You

You were our armour
No arrow could pierce

Our judge our jury
No temper as fierce
Throughout life's challenge
You've been our need
Weaker in word
Much stronger in deed
You were our strength
Without—we fear
Always close
But never too near
Irremovable irresistible
Resolute of mind
Conversely
Caring
Irreverent sympathetic
Demonstrably kind
You were our hope
Our future
On whom we could all depend
Our rights our wrongs
Judgements upheld
Or would vehemently defend
Exploited but proud
Indiscretions sometimes too loud
You were a master of fun
But as a successful parent
We're all agreed—job done

# Write On Time

How vulnerable and exposed
You leave me
On the battlefield of life
Against the enemy of time
And inevitability
You were immortal titanic
The folly of thought
And hope against time
Why after so long
Does life seem ephemeral
Time is a fraudster A trickster
Who makes for happiness short and shallow
And pain so long and deep
Time is the gaoler
And we merely prisoners
Eventually to be released
In the sum of life
Time takes away
But he gave us you
For just a short time
But it was the best time

I sat and waited for Dad to read both poems and then came a period of silence.

"Well, what do you think of them?" I couldn't wait any longer for a reply.

"They're great son, a great tribute, but as I read them, I can't help thinking I'm already dead!"

"Ah, yes, I thought you might think that. They are eulogies Dad and can be read out at funerals, but eulogy means 'good words' in Greek. They can be delivered in speech or writing, in praise of someone. They're not to be confused with 'elegy' which is a poem of serious reflection, typically a lament for the dead. I could write an elegy for your arse because that *has* already died."

"Fair point son, but you could still read them out at my funeral."

"Even if they were elegies Dad, I still would like you to know what we think of you before you go. It's not often people have a chance to read their own eulogy or elegy. Too often people get to say the right things about the ones they love when it's too late for them to hear anything!"

"Good point, son."

That Christmas down at Babs and Trix's (Richard Bell- hence 'Trixie'… it's how Barbara's mind works) farmhouse, as well as the book of poetry, I gave Reg a toy monkey, which laughed maniacally and farted when you pressed its hand. Unlike the anthology, I couldn't grapple it from his grasp! He laughed continuously throughout the holiday, pressing this cuddly toy's hand repeatedly, to the point where everyone else was taken to the point of distraction! Eighty-eight years old, and he would still prefer this kind of entertainment, to a West End play, which he sat through once, snoring audibly and continuously; much to the discomfort of others around him, including us and the annoyance of the performers.

# Chapter Fifteen

As youngsters, we didn't have many pets; the odd hamster called 'Sandy' or 'Pepper', which didn't seem to last much longer than a can of salmon that Ruth kept 'for an occasion', which she would allow us to look at briefly before returning to the dark confines of the cupboard, after tormenting us with an empty promise to 'open it soon'. In fact, much later, when returning from the Arabian desert after working there for a year, I espied a later hoarded can of salmon and without asking, availed myself of the contents. Upon finding her expensive 'treat' missing, Ruth openly and manifestly voiced displeasure over her frugality being violated, until I promised to replace it with a year's supply.

In addition, I promised to replace her 'economical' 'Rich Tea', dry-as-dust biscuits with Christmas time only 'Chocolate Digestives'. In fact, I took her shopping shortly after the commando raid on her cupboard and flung all forms of indulgence into the trolley, which wildly disturbed her sense of severe self-discipline and asceticism, brought about by necessary economic drives. My reckless shopping spree, inspired by my newly acquired, if short-lived wealth, didn't pass muster with Ruth's longer-term economic outlook or plan. And of course, ultimately, she was right!

Nevertheless, after watching the second or third hamster die of boredom following a marathon run on its 'circle of life' or more appropriately, 'wheel of death', Mum and Dad agreed to have a pet-loss-and-pain-free household once again. That was until Reg decided to bring home a parakeet, and I don't mean a budgerigar. This creature was considerably bigger and a much noisier, shriek-piercing member of the avian species. Its cage enclosure looked too small and confining, which required us to release the occupant frequently for exercise.

When not flying about like a marauding pterodactyl, it wreaked havoc on Ruth's curtains and beloved collection of 'Children's Encyclopaedia', leaving holes everywhere in its wake. Its walnut-breaking beak was terrifying; often drawing blood when any of us tried to get near it.

In fact, it is widely known that pets like these only acknowledge one owner and that became Reg, when one day, he opened and forced his great glove-covered ham-fist into the cage and gently stroked the bird's chest feathers. Initially, he got one or two painful nips but persisted until the bird released a ridiculous and pathetic sound of contentment. Moreover, it gradually acquired the ability to mimic the spoken word! Frequently, we would hear in a high-pitched outburst the 'dulcet tones' of 'Reg, Reg, Reg'... 'It's Molly on the phone'... 'Reg says bugger off!'

Reg deeply resented the times when Molly would ask Ruth if... 'he would like a cup of tea?' or ... 'Would he like something to eat?', when he was present!

"Tell her I am here and can speak for myself you know."

Children, as well as Reg, were to be seen and not heard.

Molly's approach—unaware of being ahead of her time—would have been acceptable and correct in this woke or nonbinary society, especially if she had invited Sam Smith to tea, "Would *they* like a drink?"

Visitors were often treated to an unsolicited tirade of abuse or a stuka-type dive-bombing experience, that left them either frantically trying to dodge the offending attacker or worse, wiping packages of flying bird-shit from their clothing.

Eventually and understandably, Percy, *yes Percy*, was kept to the confines of his cage during visits, but he certainly became a close and beloved member of the family; that is, right up to the inevitable moment of his demise. Years later, Reg came downstairs to find Percy lying motionless on his back with his claws facing upwards, having adopted a pose of post-mortem rigidity. Stupidly, I asked Reg if he was dead and quite expectedly and unsurprisingly, he replied, "Well, I don't think he's sunbathing."

Then, again, exhibiting a level of foolishness that warranted the reply received, I asked if he was going to bury him, "No son, I'm going to stuff him and use him as a bottle-opener."

The greatest irony of all came sometime later when Reg was showing photographs of Percy to a veterinary acquaintance, who confirmed that he should have been called Priscilla or perhaps more appropriately Pecora, which is 'ewe' in Italian, as in 'F!*k You', which astonishingly, is a phrase he didn't add to his vocabulary, given so many people said it to him spontaneously after being introduced!

As a family, we didn't actively go looking for a cat as a pet, though one came looking for us.

For three days and nights, we tried to ignore the long periods of mewing and whining that came from a female tortoiseshell kitten, outside our French windows. The pathetic appeals from this feral feline eventually tugged at our heartstrings, despite continuous protestations from me, warning of long-term responsibilities. That prediction turned out to be a period of *twenty* years and amazingly would have been longer, had she not been run over by a passing car!

So, Ruth went out and fed it some leftover food, which was surprising within a household of five children and one overworked father. She golloped it down instantly, as I suppose a starving animal would.

To her credit, Ruth eventually came round to my way of thinking and suggested, or rather insisted that Reg took her to work and give her over to an associate who owned a cat sanctuary. This he duly did and came home later that evening with the said cat in a straw-lined cardboard box surrounded by 'munch' and cat litter; oh, and answering to the name of Sophie, "I just couldn't leave her," said Reg in a pathetic tone that totally won Ruth over.

"It's probably for the best," said Ruth. No, it wasn't! From that moment on, Ruth and Reg had responsibility for another mouth to feed, with a food bill outlasting our tenure!

Despite being a kitten, this brave little animal had survived the cold-hearted act of abandonment from an insensitive, thoughtless family who probably believed cats *were* just for Christmas. She must have survived on mice or suchlike because she never brought them into us as 'presents', but just merely ate them headfirst!

After a short while and a visit to the local vet, Sophie put on weight and grew a beautiful, colourful coat. Undoubtedly, she was an attractive cat, but bloody irritable, short-tempered and totally unpredictable. She didn't like being disturbed or stroked and would often show her displeasure by clawing anyone who displayed acts of warmth and kindness. She preferred acts of rough and tumble play; more a lioness than a lap cat! She also demanded to be let out at night... all night!

I remember only too well, how one morning she came into the house looking very distressed and licking her fur continuously. She jumped up onto the ironing board where I was preparing a shirt for work. This procedure often involved Reg, Peter or me ironing at least two or three shirts at any given time, as somebody else would inevitably claim ownership of a garment that one of us was ready to adorn. During our teens, we all had the same measurements.

Anyway, despite Sophie being agitated, I was in a hurry and took hold to remove her from the board. As if in slow motion, to my astonishment and horror, a *wave* of fleas... millions of the buggers, left her body and spilled across my shirt! Within seconds, they had dispersed and completely disappeared!

From that moment on and well after we kids had all gone our separate ways, Ruth and Reg never entirely got rid of them. We were bitten mercilessly whilst watching the television, in the dining room and even in bed! We sought advice and even tried to fumigate the house, to no avail. Even ten years after leaving home, I came to visit one evening and got bitten on the ankle.

Sophie must have come into contact with a dead hedgehog or something, but it was the 'gift' from her that just kept giving until the situation virtually drove us insane.

Despite this terrifying infestation, we all possess some wonderful memories of her. And if she gave us some shocks, these were reciprocated on occasions, such as the previously mentioned 'pike' incident. Sophie was probably still suffering from PTSD as a result of her piscatorial encounter with the pike in the bathroom when she discovered the twenty-three-pound, blood-soaked monster of a turkey—complete with head, neck and claws waiting for her as she came indoors—that I had just brought back from 'Smithfield Market', one Christmas Eve.

To her, it must have looked like the big daddy of all the songbirds she'd murdered, and this was retribution! We didn't see her at all over the Christmas period. It didn't look so big behind the butcher's counter and for a small fee. I could have had it prepared for the oven, instead of wrestling with it myself. All the shelves inside the oven had to be removed, as well as the bird's legs; each one a meal in itself.

Quite unexpectedly, Reg brought home another cat a couple of years later. This time a ginger tomcat. Reg decided to call him 'Tex', after the song 'Two Gun Tex from Texas' by Barry Gray and the 'Michael Holliday Orchestra'. Of course, realising my mistake afterwards, I asked why.

"Because he shoots all over the place whilst marking his territory." Why hadn't I thought of that? I should have known better than to ask.

Sophie was intolerant of him and was put out for a while, to say the least. She didn't waste any opportunity to have a swipe at his cute little face every time they passed one another. However, because he was younger, smaller and more docile, Sophie began to accept him.

Just as well—he eventually grew larger than her.

Sophie inspired me to write a poem about her in an earlier published work:

# Why Don't Cats Smile?

Why don't cats laugh?
Why don't cats smile?
Go-Cats have come-backs
Their food tastes so vile
Why don't cats smile?
Are they unable to?
Is it because we throw boots
When we really mean shoo?
Why are cats doctored
When they've got no I.Q.?
I know why cats don't laugh
If you had fleas—would you?

Many years later when Sophie died, once again I flirted recklessly with the notion that Reg could engage in a sensible conversation, by asking if he had buried her, "No, son, I've shoved a wooden handle up her arse, so that I can use her as a bog-brush!"

He definitely missed her, as too his best friend Tex, who ran up a staggering total of some twenty-plus years before departing for that great litter tray in the sky.

A little while after his loss, Reg genuinely sounded surprised when he informed me that he was getting an unusually large number of birds in the garden, "Oh, really, I wonder how that can be?" was my response, with a level of sarcasm which definitely wasn't lost on him.

# Chapter Sixteen

Fast forward to 1995 and the spring term of my fourth year in teaching, as Head of Year Eight, when a member of staff appeared, saying my father wanted to talk to me. Knowing this was extremely unusual for Reg to interrupt me in school, I quickly arranged some cover and went to see him.

He told me that he was driving to a gardening job and his van had broken down. Ordinarily, this wouldn't have been enough to bother or unsettle him. Something far more important was troubling him and as he was explaining the possible causes for its malfunction, he broke down and cried; the very first time I'd ever seen him release this kind of emotion. As I comforted him, drawing upon the skills of my training, I was still uneasily displaced by this role reversal. Dad had always been a rock, in times of trouble.

Then he mentioned Kay, my brother's fiancé, who had died several days previously.

Understandably, minor issues had become insurmountable in the wake of this family tragedy.

Over Christmas of the previous year, we had noticed a significant lump that had appeared on Kay's neck and urged her to have it investigated. It turned out to be 'Non-Hodgkin Lymphoma'.

Despite medical intervention, she quickly, over the course of the year, succumbed to the condition.

I remember visiting her in hospital during the previous September, on one of the multiple occasions she had been admitted for treatment. She looked racked with pain and discomfort, "Hi, Kay, I've brought you a present."

"Why go through that unnecessary trouble, there's nothing I need?"

I handed her a tin of baked beans with sausages. She first appeared to look quizzically at the gift and then erupted into laughter; the last time I would ever see her do so. She died the following January, within days of her proposed marriage to Pete. We were all at her bedside.

I was shocked to see her in her final hours, looking like something out of Edvard Munch's 'The Scream'. We were indebted to the kindness and caring nature of the nurses, who had made her passing as comfortable as possible. Oh, how we depend so much upon these angels!

Vicariously experiencing my brother's pain, we all were haunted by this distressful event.

Inexplicably, I was, in words taken from Vera Brittain's 'A Testament of Youth', elevated to a... 'height of articulateness'. In only ten minutes, I had written the following song and later performed it at her funeral.

## This Sweet Surrender

You've had a long hard fight
But now you have to go
Had so little time together

To share the love we know
Reach out and hold my hand
I'm here to see you through
This sweet surrender
No more tears to cry
Except for us who stay
There's an end to all the suffering
For those who go away
I'll never leave your side
I'm here to see you through
This sweet surrender
Please Don't wait for me
Even though my heart is breaking
As I look at you and see
All the pain that you are taking
Please don't wait for me
You'll find a place
Where there's eternal love
Now there's no more light
And winter seems much colder
For those you leave behind forever
Each year as we grow older
Our love will never die
We're here to see you through
This sweet surrender

# Chapter Seventeen

Whilst I was undergoing teacher training, money was always in short supply and Reg would sometimes produce a 'Jerry Can' of petrol that he had managed to bring back from the trips to Scotland, his company sometimes sent him on. On occasions, when he filled up the three-tonner, he sploshed some 'juice' into the empty petrol can to bring home. He said it was provided by the 'generosity' of the company. I'm convinced that they would have been less than generous had they known, but for me, it certainly came at a time of need. Although I tried not to take it for granted, it was a well and gratefully received perk.

However, during his excursions to the far north, he never missed an opportunity in his spare time to play darts with the locals, who had great respect for his level of skill. Frequently, he would be challenged to a game and would dominate the board; only losing when the effects of alcohol overcame him, as defeated players bought him a round.

These Scots were dockers and tough as old boots. They were generous but didn't tolerate 'Sassenachs' gladly. Reg had earned the respect to be amongst them, but even so, at times—and although hard to believe—he overstepped the mark. As in the case one evening when he entered his 'local' in Aberdeen to take on all-comers. He enquired as to where one of the locals was. The barman informed him that he would be in shortly but advised Reg not to mention how Aberdeen Football Club had fared in the recent game because they lost, and he always became irascible and unpredictable when this happened.

"Thanks for the tip-off," said Reg and went back to his game.

Reg noticed his arrival and after purchasing his pint the local came over to the board with a long face.

"Ooh, you don't look happy, did Aberdeen lose then?" said Reg with all the sensitivity of a hyena.

"Aye, dinnae mention it!"

"Oh, sorry to hear that... three-nil, wasn't it?"

"I said dinnae mention it!"

They played the first leg of darts which Reg easily won and then turned to the local and said, "Well, you lost that one... just like Aberdeen."

"Shut yer geggy sassenach!" came the reply.

At this point, Reg was only too aware that his ill-advised comments were striking home and decided to ease off as the local went to buy more drinks.

The next two legs went the same way as the first and Reg claimed the match. By this stage, the Aberdeen fan had consumed two more pints and was at best irritated, but was veritably incandescent at Reg's next quip, "Well, you lost three-nil there, a bit like Aberdeen then?"

Looks of incredulity came from the faces of the other locals and the barman who could see what was coming.

The Aberdeen supporter's face became contorted with rage as spittle and invective spewed from his lips.

"Dinnae say that y'wee jobby!"

"Time to leave Reg!" advised one of the locals.

Reg bid them all a good night and as he reached the door, he turned to the Aberdeen supporter and said, "Aberdeen play football like you play darts!"

At this, the supporter became apoplectic with rage and momentarily incapacitated by his temper.

Reg was out of the pub like a shot and had barely shut the door before the first-pint mug smashed into it, followed in quick succession by the second and third. An almighty argument erupted behind it as tempers flared and voices were raised. He hurriedly returned to his hotel. The next night he had the temerity to return to the pub as if nothing had happened.

The barman was not best pleased, "I told you not to mention Aberdeen!"

"I know, but I didn't think he would react like that. He was a bit tetchy. Where is he?"

"He's been banned, as you will be if you do that again!"

"Understood," said Reg. "Anyone for a game of darts?"

# Chapter Eighteen

Christmas was a very special time for us as a family, living on a housing estate in Borehamwood. It wasn't your archetypal Dickensian setting, and it probably only snowed twice there in thirty years on Christmas Eve or Day, but the special element within the occasion was indeed the family.

As children, the excitement grew early with the build-up from school plays and brass band rehearsals. I distinctly remember arriving home in the dark winter evenings and sitting with Mum, listening to carols on the radio.

For all of us except Claire, it was a mile-and-a-half walk to school. How she was never enrolled in the same secondary school as the other four of us, was a complete mystery. I suspect it may have had something to do with a late form submission or a change in local authority policy. Even help from the lead singer of the band in which I too, was a performer, didn't change the outcome, and he was the local labour candidate!

Initially, it was hard for Claire to attend a different and quite honestly, publicly perceived inferior school, but in truth, three of us had either left or were about to leave ours anyway.

Additionally and perhaps more fortuitously, she didn't have to endure the times we got absolutely drenched, whilst walking to school in poor weather; in itself a good reason not to follow us.

Nevertheless, the season of goodwill was always memorable for us and Ruth and Reg always supported our community interests at this time; attending shows, assemblies and award ceremonies.

The one aspect of Christmas that I do remember as a child is that our parents never put up decorations or trees until Christmas Eve. As youngsters, we would love making the paperchains that adorned our living-room ceiling, which over the years became pitted with drawing-pin holes. For most years, the smell of the real pine tree filled our nostrils with the scent of the season. That was until the mid-seventies when plastic and foil fake trees became more fashionable, along with the hideously gaudy, ruff-like ceiling decorations. In fairness, it wasn't too long before we reinstated the real pine tree due to a unanimous vote.

At this time in our lives, out of school, Christmas was indeed and quite rightly confined to December. It's not just because I've become much older and more like Victor Meldrew in my ways, that I think Christmas now comes too early. Think about it, when teaching, we tried to keep the children focused on the curriculum, as far into the autumn term as possible. Struggling parents didn't want the financial burden that came from the demands of their children, after being targeted by commercial advertising in October. For me, there is a more sombre and powerful reason why Christmas celebrations should not be seen or heard of until the twelfth month—Remembrance Day! I find it unacceptable and disrespectful, to hear and see companies flogging Christmas stock on 11$^{th}$ November.

As kids, Reg and Ruth always drummed into us the importance of Remembrance Day and how we should always observe the two-minute silence. This salutation was made even more solemn, with the thunderous sound of the guns being fired in London thirteen miles away to mark the event.

As a head teacher, I always made Remembrance Day a point of reference on the calendar and ensured my pupils were accustomed to the service. Each year the British Legion made a guest appearance in the school hall. This I felt was particularly appropriate given that we had lost one of our former pupils in combat.

I know that Reg and Ruth both feel the occasion has gained even more poignancy with the regrettable loss of lives in more recent theatres of war, but there is still a great deal of ignorance amongst people, particularly of the younger non-serving generations, who have not been brought up to acknowledge such terrible loss.

On Thursday, 11$^{th}$ November 2021, Gwynneth and I were out walking with some friends Andy and Jill, when remembering Mum and Dad's request that I pay respect, suggested that we stop on the top of a hill and reflect. At exactly 11:00, we stood still and peered across the view, accompanied by our thoughts. Halfway through the silence, a man in his late twenties—early thirties came mountain-biking down a well-signposted track prohibiting cycling. In our peripheral vision, we heard and saw him struggling to get his bike over the style, mumbling about the lack of help. As he drew level with us, he had the bare-faced temerity to say, "Am I completely invisible?"

"No, you're ignorant, we're observing the two-minute silence!" I wasn't as bothered about the cycling infringement as my walking partner was.

To his credit, he did apologise, but then raced off *before* the period of silence had elapsed, having duly disrupted our observance.

The mother of the late Baroness Shirley Williams, Vera Brittain, greatly inspired my writing. Her novel 'Testament of Youth' is not an easy book to read, both for its elaborate and demanding language and of course its harrowing accounts of World War I. The following poem is a tribute to her and all serving ranks who paid the ultimate price, for our peace:

## The Death of Reason

(A Remembrance Poem)

With pounding heart
Heaving breast and panting lung
He runs
For death beckons and awaits

His or other's life
It matters not
Inexorably the moment comes
Irreversibly irretrievably
The moment arrives

The cold Earth receives her son
Littered and strewn with torn flesh

And stained with life's blood

All joy all youth hope and reason
Are crushed gone lost—forever

Disturbingly, though thankfully not the case now, whenever Reg, Ruth and I watch their grandsons play premiership cricket, or football we can't help but mention that if this was 1914, or 1940 they would be off to war in their 'Old Pals' battalions, or embroiled in 'dogfights' over Kent.

With much excitement, even as teenagers we loved the spirit of Christmas. We would be sent off to bed with great expectations and would each discover a pillowcase overflowing with presents at the foot of the bed the next morning. Reg and Ruth would make us wonderful toys when we were younger and even though we had to share some, to this day I wonder how they managed to keep the dream alive, with so little cash to spare. As we got older, the gift of giving was even better than the receiving. For me, presents on Christmas Day were sacred, and I would often splash all my cash on those special ephemeral moments.

Sure, I always felt 'the pinch' well after the season was finished, but I never spent more than I had. However, I fully understand how people become victims of their own generosity and selflessness and recognise the practicalities and prudence of waiting until the 'Sales', which of course are always on now. To us Christmasphiles though, there is nothing quite like the time of year; even if Coca-Cola did invent the over-inflated, wellington-booted, scarlet-clothed and lengthy, white-bearded character that we associate with the occasion.

Even now, Reg and Ruth spend not a small amount of time putting together a homemade sledge full of modest, individually wrapped gifts, to give to their children, grandchildren and no doubt now, their great-grandchildren. Wrapped up in that small token of love, carefully selected on a frugal budget, is the true message of Christmas. That cheap bottle of shower gel or unrequired scarf means as much to me as a combined hammer and bottle-opener that I received from my South African friends, or indeed some self-made cards from our kids or grandchildren.

Conversely, we never really possessed the same amount of excitement or appreciation as Reg over his seasonal homemade beer, which had the unique odour of used washing-up water! It never tasted anything like the 'Adnams Bitter' in the polypins I bought. It tasted like cabbage water, providing the same effects but was certainly not as beneficial. He had no hope whatsoever of replicating the taste of even the worst type of gassy, tinned or bottled beer of the time, with those awful seventies do-it-yourself kits. He would go through the meticulous, though unrewarding process, of making our house smell like a brewery yard and ending up with the same explosive crap *every* time.

How could he ever have imagined that his extensive efforts would create anything other than fizzy dishwater? Every bloody year spawned another vintage of this offensive tipple. He would systematically clean and fill a multitude of demi-johns with this obnoxious fluid and then store the lot in a cupboard under the stairs to ferment. Frequently, we would all be shocked out of our skins by exploding corks going off like mortars; only to be replaced by Reg until the next time, a short while later.

For some inexplicable reason, our next-door neighbour loved the stuff, although I feel this level of adulation was extended to anyone generous enough to give him something for nothing! He was always scrounging around for a free drink and would always put his request in for a sample of the new batch, which was inevitably, always as bad as the last. He must have suffered from Rhinitis, or—judging by his 'grog-blossom'—alcoholism, to want repeat deliveries of this industrial cleaning fluid!

Albert would always turn up uninvited for his reserved batch, but on this one occasion, Reg decided that he would personally go around and deliver this present himself. This flagged up a sense of jiggery-pokery at the time, especially as Reg said that he was going to give this 'special jar of beer' to Albert tight-arse.

"Why special?" I ruefully asked.

"Because I've given it a damn good shaking and I know he's just finished decorating his lounge."

*Is this a good idea?* I thought as I followed Reg up his neighbour's garden path and to his front door on which he rapped out his arrival. Before Albert answered the door, Reg impishly gave the jar of beer another good shake, whilst forcing his thumb over the cork.

Albert was of course ecstatic to receive the expected gift but was equally excited to show off his newly decorated lounge, with expensive 'Anaglypta' textured wallpaper and tacky polystyrene ceiling tiles, which were all the rage at the time. I say all the *rage*, they were until people realised they were the cause of raging fires in their homes. In fact, they gave a new sinister and literal meaning to the phrase 'Come home to a *real* fire' that was made popular when we were youngsters, ironically, by a coal advert.

I suppose these hideous tiles were the internal equivalent of latter-day exterior cladding and likewise should have been certified unsafe before they cost lives as an unstable accelerant.

With the look of smugness still on his face at the completion of his endeavours and feeling of one-upmanship, Albert carefully placed the demi-jar on his coffee table and continued to wax lyrical over his D.I.Y. craftmanship.

Suddenly, there was an almighty explosion, which even surprised those of us who were expecting it. Albert had the look of a shell-shocked war veteran and simultaneously adopted the pose of someone who looked like they had soiled themself.

The bullet-like cork went through one of the recently glued tiles, whilst the content distributed itself over the new wallpaper, carpet and us! The coverage somehow seemed to exceed the amount in the bottle. Albert's wife came in and screamed… "What the hell has happened?"

If Albert hadn't soiled himself before, he must have done then!

Almost incredulously, Albert surveyed the war-torn battlefield of what used to be his lounge, whilst his wife disappeared hurriedly to find cleaning materials.

Fighting back the overwhelming urge to laugh, Reg said that we'd best be on our way as Ruth had got tea on, "We'll see ourselves out then Albert. If you need a top-up, just let me know."

Albert was far too distracted by the carnage that had just ransacked his home, to reply.

One could easily hear the subsequent exchange of vitriol between him and his wife through our dividing wall.

I can only remember once going back into their house after that affair and if we did, the offer to return certainly didn't come from Dorothy! However, Albert got his own back on Reg and me.

It was the New Year celebrations just prior to my twenty-first birthday and Albert invited us all into his place.

Drinks were flowing and food was plentiful, but for some reason, known only to a young, inexperienced, uninitiated and immature buffoon like me, I thought it would be amusing to pilfer people's drinks whilst they weren't looking and 'neck' them in succession. It didn't occur to me that I was imbibing a horrific concoction of alcoholic 'paralysis' but it certainly was humorous to see the expressions of bewilderment and hear the confused comments of partygoers, relieved of their newly-charged vessels.

It didn't take Albert long to realise what I was up to and appeared to act surprised when his drinks vanished but quickly acquired replacements and put them down with his back turned as a temptation. He even mixed up the beverages and waited patiently for me to fall into his trap. After poaching his latest short, he would look around and put on a beguiling display of mock disbelief, before asking for or collecting another drink.

It wasn't long before I felt as if I was standing quite still and the house and its occupants were moving around me. Lights began to flash and the individual conversations merged into one cacophony of deafening noise. The alarm bells of imminent 'chunder' were pealing as I set off on what seemed a long journey home. My only recollection of that departure was imagining myself on stage in a production of Swan Lake and pirouetting with all the grace of Rudolph Nureyev.

In essence, I bounced off most surfaces between me and my bed and didn't even get undressed before getting into it! In fact, I only managed to get onto it. Pulling back the sheets involved one extra effort that I certainly wasn't prepared to undertake.

On reflection, one last extra effort that I should have made was to make myself vomit and force copious amounts of water down me before succumbing to the effects of binge drinking!

When I finally surfaced the next morning—and I use the term advisedly—as well as the pain from my head, which felt like an evil gremlin was trying to dig his way out, I was aware of being surrounded by a 'pond' of evil-smelling soup. It was *everywhere*! And it had all come out of me. I had been sick in my sleep. How I hadn't drowned in this putrid poisonous potion of feckless wilfulness still haunts and terrifies me today!

Rightly so, with my head banging like a marching band's base drum, Ruth made me wash and clean every bit of bedding and carpeted area that had been contaminated, as well as the bunk-bed frame.

It took me several days to fully recover and much, much longer to rid the bedroom of stale vomit.

That'll teach you, said Reg unsympathetically. Why, I don't know because he didn't exactly come out of this bonanza of binge drinking any better off than me. Mum found him on the stairs the next morning and managed to mumble out a greeting of 'Morning Duc' before Ruth, rather ruthlessly and repeatedly, hit him over the head with the unslept-on pillow that she woke up to.

Albert had confided in Reg over my behaviour at the party, whilst plying him with vast quantities of his own dreadful beer, before following these up with neat whisky chasers.

The next day, Albert must have thought, *all's square again*, as he smugly dusted his hands.

# Chapter Nineteen

As well as being brilliant at subtracting from five-0-one, over the years Reg has become quite adept at completing crossword puzzles; and I don't mean the 'coffee-time' quick-as-you-like to complete varieties. Oh no, he prefers to tackle the much more challenging cryptic ones which have clues that read like a spy's coded message:

Clue—'Wave cereal bowl' (8). Answer—Brandish.

Clue—'Damp fog hides nothing' (5). Answer—Moist… *What*?

Now, I'm not going to leave you without solutions to these because you may wish to join the Secret Service one day and spend the whole of your life tackling this kind of problem-solving, working from Government Communications Headquarters (GCHQ) with no hope whatsoever of finding a partner. Look at 'Morse'—solved many crimes, could do the Times Crossword every day in four minutes flat and sadly couldn't hold down a relationship.

Right, Cereal = bran, bowl=dish. Therefore, the answer is 'brandish' or another word for wave.

Another word for fog is mist. If you hide nothing or '0' in the mist you get the answer 'moist'.

Devilishly clever and chuffing annoying to the inexperienced or untutored quizzer!

So, despite being so proficient or accomplished at crosswords, why on earth did he foster in us as kids, the wrong terminology or pronunciation of certain words, which came to embarrass me during my professional career?

Now don't get me wrong, the late, great Dylan Thomas uses many linguistic techniques to conjure up a powerful description as he takes the reader through an imaginative journey of 'Under Milk Wood'. Phrases such as 'bible-black, sloeblack, crowblack' or 'fishingboat bobbing sea' are excellent examples of portmanteau. In Reg's case, he just mispronounced words with the malapropistic fluency of Hilda Baker. His habitual misuse of words had a lasting effect on the unsuspecting ears of his impressionable children.

I recall at my first ever staff meeting as acting head, delivering a sentence with the word 'cleansiness' in it and being told by a member of staff, that I probably meant 'cleanliness'.

I couldn't tell her that my father taught me this absurd variation, so I merely replied that she was right, and it was a slip of the tongue.

On an earlier occasion in the same school, I referred to an elephant as a 'ptachyderm' and was duly and embarrassingly corrected with the word 'pachyderm'. When I confronted Reg over these mispronunciations, he merely replied, "Well, I'm not as *edumacated* as you."

My reply was… "But I am just as uneducated as you, and I'm a bloody teacher!"

"My head corrected my incorrect use of the English language."

"Well, son, it wasn't your head that made the correction, it was someone else's," said Mr Pun!

Reg would say 'sospan' instead of 'saucepan'. His reasoning, "Well, we say 'sosages', we don't say 'saucesages' (sausages)."

He also *taught* us to say 'eggcelerator' when teaching us to drive, which sounds nothing like 'accelerator' but more like a Heath Robinson invention that encouraged hens to lay faster.

It's taken me and my siblings years to jettison this linguistic 'baggage' from our repertoires, but in spite of the irregularities to this daft, doublespeak gibberish, one can't help thinking that there is an element of rational thought linked to it. Then again, I think he just puts the 'dick' in 'dictionary'!

One thing is for sure, his use of language to cold-callers is an example of theatrical genius.

When a dubious caller attempts to con my father out of his hard-earned savings, he often adopts a very child-like, high-pitched voice and says, "I'm on my own, Mummy and Daddy are not in at the moment, but I can take a message."

That approach generally gets the right response and the caller hangs up. Amazingly, there have been occasions when *legitimately* concerned callers have worried about a very young child being left at home on their own and have asked him questions in a worried tone, "How old are you?"

"Three."

"Three? Well, I'm three in two sleeps." This is often followed by a pause of incredulity, "Well, when are your parents back?"

"I don't know this time; they've gone to the pub again." (Said with fake but convincing crying.)

"Don't cry, just call 999."

To which, Reg replied in his own voice, "That's exactly what I propose to do with the information you gave me in your introduction."

Click … whirrrrr.

His other preferred method of engagement is to talk absolute gibberish at an incredible speed.

"Me-udder-sigger-hidder-mugger-wugger."

The baffled caller came back with, "I'm sorry?"

And Dad replied, "Are you deaf? I said quite clearly, me-udder-sigger-hidder-mugger-wugger!"

"You stupid twat!" said the caller, to which Reg replies, "So you can read minds as well?"

Only recently, he was heard answering a fraudulent caller, who insisted that Reg and Ruth had something wrong with their internet connection, which needed to be addressed on their computer.

"Oh, you must be mistaken," said Reg.

"Oh no," came the insistent reply. "We must check it."

"Well, we're not on the internet… we're on the outer net and the only computer I've got is an abacus." This was closely followed by a barrage of invective, which must have warmed up the cold-caller's ears.

When I've called Reg and said, "Hi, Dad, are you well?"
He'll say, "I is, I is, but I can't be sure."
"What do you mean, you can't be sure if you're well?"
"No, I can't be sure if I'm your dad."

I've said to him on more than one occasion "You're unbelievable. My son has a degree and because of listening to you, is talking gibberish like a village idiot!"

"He am, he am."

More recently, during his eighty-eighth year, Reg suffered a stroke and lost the ability to speak, and it nearly broke our hearts to see him struggle to communicate. To see his palpable anger, despair and frustration rise, with a solitary tear running down his cheek, as he fought in vain to recover his power of speech, was humbling. It was emotionally draining for us all, especially as we knew his brother John never recovered from his stroke, but Reg is a fighter and didn't succumb.

It wasn't any religious faith that made me kiss him, grip his hand and tell him to relax and be patient, whilst longing for him to say something—*anything*! It was love, pure and simple that gave me the belief that he could hold on and come back to us.

As I left him for the night, he gripped my hand and gestured for a pencil. He scribbled something down and handed it to me… it said, "Take care, son."

## Teardrop

In that tear
I behold all that is dear to me
In itself a world of emotion
Packed with joy and despair
Anger laughter and sorrow
In that tear
I see all that is significant and precious

In a greater and lesser world outside
In that tear
I see love
And a drop of hope
In that tear
I see a reflection of us both

Incredibly, within three days, his ability to speak returned, as if his brain had rewired itself and redirected electrical paths. There were some minor changes, but almost undetectable.

Never were we all more grateful for the healing qualities of modern medical intervention.

When I heard him speak again, my heart soared which prompted me to comment, "There you are, the stroke left no lasting effect. You were speaking gibberish then, and you still are. It must have been hard for the doctors to diagnose your condition."

"Well, I didn't need to ask for a bedpan; they definitely knew when I needed one!"

# Chapter Twenty

My sisters Barbara and Angie, in partnership with their husbands—who have clearly been suckers for punishment—have organised numerous fishing breaks with Reg and Ruth, whether on canals or in accommodation near lakes.

Ruth inexplicably to the layman, likes to fish on moving water such as rivers or canals and is quite happy to constantly recast her line as the flow repeatedly brings back the float or takes it out of sight. I think it's the challenge, after all, she married Reg.

Despite having boated on canals in the past and not stopped at Birmingham—if you get my drift—it's strange how anglers like themselves have little patience for other leisure pursuits on the water. Both Ruth and Reg will state the case that boats, dogs and swimmers disturb the fish, whereas playing or pulling fish towards the bank with a barbed hook stuck in their lip and then having to gasp for oxygen whilst disgorgement is taking place, doesn't!

There are few times when Ruth hasn't been disturbed or embarrassed by Reg whilst fishing, but on one occasion she supported his response and felt his frustration, whilst they were fishing their club's stretch of the canal.

Their captain had failed to tell them in advance, that a large canoeing fraternity was due to pass, so when it did unexpectedly it was the source of much consternation amongst the disturbed anglers. As they paddled by, there was much splashing, noise, shouting and worse, entanglement with fishing lines. Appeals from the disrupted anglers were ignored and words were exchanged between the two parties; especially when one boat capsized and Reg made no attempt to help the occupants as they struggled to the bank but laughed raucously. When the drenched pair finally made it to the bank, they slipped and struggled to extract themselves, which just made Reg laugh louder.

"Why didn't you help us?" said one of them.

"Because you're doing nothing to help us. You look like a seal in that outfit... an imbecile!"

Then a canoe with a single occupant came past and complained to Reg that the water was moving too slowly, "Isn't there any flow on this water?"

"Well, every Tom, Dick and Harry is on this stretch, so I don't see why there shouldn't be a 'Flo' as well!" replied Reg.

More recently, both parents have experienced difficulties in carrying their fishing equipment; much less being able to attend working parties for their clubs where they are now honorary life members.

On several occasions, I have been invited with Gwynneth and the kids for the day, to visit their locations. Conversely, to watch Ruth at her sport is gratifying. Without a doubt, she is an accomplished angler and is in her element on the banks or aboard boats. She sits so patiently and motionless; transfixed on her bobbing float, waiting for it to disappear and tug at the tip of her rod. Then, strike and gently bring the fish home, after giving it enough slack to run and wear itself out. Out of her peripheral vision, she would seize the landing net and talk softly in reassuring tones to the landed fish, as if it could understand.

As a youngster, my son Harry would sit next to Reg, with a rod set up for him. Harry was interested in wildlife and enjoyed watching the swifts dive and skim across the surface of the water with great agility, catching flies and midges.

During one of these idyllic moments and a prolonged discussion on birds, Reg asked Harry if he had heard of the elusive 'Brown-tailed Warbler'.

"People have only heard these birds in the wild but surprisingly, have never seen them."

Gripped with interest at this statement, Harry asked Reg if they might see one on that day.

"You'll have to sit very quietly and listen for its call. It's very distinctive and recognisable."

Whilst Harry was concentrating hard on his motionless float, Reg lifted up his right leg in a typical act of accentuating his intentions—honestly, he could have been a 'Tiller' dancer—and emitted a voluminous, concussive 'ripper', that not only momentarily shocked but also unseated Harry.

"That was it, Harry! That was the Brown-tailed Warbler. Did you see it?"

"I certainly heard it, Grandpops!"

Reg was incapacitated by his own laughter. He was finding it very difficult to draw breath and recover any sense of composure.

Later that day Harry shared his newly adopted means of imitating the sound of the brown-tailed warbler (aka Reg) with his mother.

"Honestly, Reg, you're incorrigible and a pleb!"

"What's a pleb?" said Reg, giving the false impression that he knew what the former meant!

It's probably worth mentioning that inevitably due to her sport's sedentary nature, Ruth did in fact put on some weight. Consequently, she was encouraged and decided to attend a 'Weight-Watchers course. To her credit Ruth was persistent in following the suggestions of her tutors; so much so that she did indeed reach her desired weight, but for some extraordinary reason her body's natural metabolism was put out of kilter and the gradual slimming process didn't slow down. As the weeks passed, Ruth was rapidly taking on the appearance of an anorexia cachexia or wasting syndrome sufferer. She was worried as we all were, but luckily her doctor was able to reverse the problem by getting her back onto a normal diet regime.

Of course, like the rest of us Reg was terribly displaced, but once through the ordeal, it didn't stop him putting up a surgeon's skeletal model, with a large label attached around its neck, with the words: 'Ruth's Goal Weight'

# Chapter Twenty-One

Reg has always had an extreme aversion to snakes. Even coming into proximity with a draft excluder or an overly large bratwurst can trigger a fit of hysterics; strange, when you think that he has never come across a venomous one at home or during his limited excursions abroad, to places like Scotland and Wales. I could understand this otherwise rational behaviour if he had met a king cobra or coral snake in a jungle setting whilst on covert duties with the 'Chindits' or on a crusade with Indiana Jones, but not whilst he was serving as a military policeman in Baden-Baden.

I'll admit that the thought of happening upon an adder unexpectedly, fills me with a sense of trepidation, but I should still be fascinated with this encounter. The chances of Reg ever seeing one when he was more active were slim then; almost non-existent now. I can only surmise that he must have had a life-changing episode with a pet python-adorned belly dancer at some 'stag'-do that left him traumatised.

Nevertheless, I remember vividly an incident at a gardening job in Chorleywood, where, as youngsters, Pete and I were helping Dad clear a plot for vegetables.

All was well until Dad turned over a large stone to reveal what I could easily identify today as a nest of slow worms. These are not even snakes, but harmless and legless reptiles.

What followed next can only be described as a terrifying and macabre incident, with all the sinister, gory and gruesome outcomes of a chainsaw massacre. Reg hopped from leg to leg in his wellied feet as if manipulated by a Punch and Judy puppeteer, with all the height and flexibility of a floor gymnast, whilst screaming out blasphemous phrases on a soprano's register. What at first appeared very amusing to us, quickly became a scene of horror, as Reg wielding his spade like that of a mediaeval knight's sword, dispatched the majority of those poor creatures which—as their name suggests—weren't quick enough to get away.

What was left, to our young, frightened and impressionable eyes looked like a bloody mass of 'chum'; the ground bait thrown overboard by anglers to lure large game fish. What, in the name of all that is holy would have made him think that these elegant creatures could have caused him harm? I'm no Chris Packham, but I'm sure at his age I would have known that there was only one indigenous snake whose venom was harmful to humans, and it was probably on holiday, sunning itself on a rocky outcrop in the South Downs.

Reg was bathed in dripping sweat after his 'ordeal' and was mumbling, if not gibbering, incomprehensibly. It took some time for him to regain a level of sanity that even we could recognise. The look of abject fear on his face was not the result of surveying the carnage of his frenzied endeavours, but rather not knowing where the two that escaped were. He surveyed the land around him with his spade, like a sapper would gently prod the sand looking for anti-tank or personnel mines. He even held up his hand to silence us as he monitored the ground as if we should break his concentration.

This indeed was the act of a truly disturbed man. His manic disposition did not change until we left the job. He even left his drink and biscuits, provided by the customer, who shared her concerns for his wellbeing. Pete and I availed ourselves of them instead.

Apparently, this wasn't the only encounter with a 'snake' that Reg had endured. Rewinding to the Monday, following his marriage on the Saturday back in '53 and still on honeymoon, he decided to go fishing locally whilst Ruth stayed home and did some laundry. This of course was the expected role of any housewife at the time.

However, Reg probably had some premonition that one day his wife might be better than him at this sport and therefore 'tied' her to the stove and washing barrel, to avoid embarrassment. Nevertheless, after spending approximately two hours catching nothing he decided to pack up and return to *his newly married wife!* As he left the lake to walk down the path to the main road, he says that a 'large' grass snake slithered across the track, causing him to panic and leap onto a gate, from which he fell but immediately regained his perch in a single movement.

It is truly baffling, that he might have identified a grass snake in the wild back in 1953 but failed to recognise a harmless species twenty-odd years later.

He says it was only a two- or three-minute walk to the road along this path but his thorough surveillance of the outlying area took him twenty minutes! Did he think it was going to slither up his trouser leg to seek refuge in his underpants?

When he got home, the look of distress was still clearly visible on his face. Ruth tried to be sympathetic and humour his needs but had a sheet to wring out through the rollers of a hand-operated wringer. They certainly had the amenities of a well-equipped modern house. She asked Reg to turn the handle whilst she fed it through. As she bent down to pick up the sheet, Reg, preoccupied with his story of 'life and death', started to turn the handle before she was ready and caught her hair in the rollers.

Oblivious to her predicament, Reg continued to turn the handle until he heard her screams. At this point, shocked back into reality, he reversed the wheel at precisely the same time that Ruth frantically grasped hold of the rollers on the other side of the machine; ironically, trapping her fingers. The ensuing barrage of obscenities, not only jogged Reg's mind back into reality but also made him wonder if he had ever dated a trooper before she married an idiot!

"Sod the bloody snake, get me out of this bloody contraption!" constituted some of the printable language exchanged.

Reg had to painstakingly take the wringer apart because he couldn't turn the rollers either way without making Ruth's situation worse.

Many years later, whilst reminiscing with my parents, I asked Reg if he had ever considered that getting bitten by a ferocious dog was more likely than receiving a fatal snake bite in this country. Before he could answer, Ruth said, "He was bitten by a dangerous dog, but they put the wrong animal down!"

# Chapter Twenty-Two

Back in his prime, Reg was very fit, sporty and popular due to his physical characteristics and wit. My son Harry takes after him in all these departments—not to mention a few others—and is an accomplished cricketer to boot. I'm sure the power and strength come from his grandfather. He is tall and like Reg has hands like JCB buckets. All these attributes have made him a successful player.

Reg unlike Harry never received formal coaching in any discipline, but he did enjoy playing cricket for his firm, the Sun Printers in Watford. Occasionally, as youngsters, we would accompany him to some of his matches. To be fair Reg was considered the 'blacksmith' of the team. He enjoyed the principle of the game, which involved hitting something very hard. Although he didn't have the technical command of his grandson, he nevertheless had good hand/eye coordination.

Unfortunately, because of his colour blindness, he became confused between the red and green spectrums. This is particularly difficult when someone is trying to knock your block off, with a red missile against a background of grass and trees, with the only protection being a faded, sweat-stained cap! Whilst fielding, he often lost the ball in plain sight. Imagine how much worse it could have been had he been a bomb disposal technician or even a common or garden electrician? "Red to earth and blew to bits!"

Anyway, when Reg went into bat, he usually hit a couple of sixes or fours and then was out because he had no inkling of how to defend a good delivery or nudge the ball down legside for a single.

He had to borrow all his equipment which often wasn't the correct size, including the bats but as far as the latter was concerned, he preferred to wield a smaller and lighter one, as the 'pick-up' on the earlier, heavy bats wasn't as effective as it is today on carefully weight distributed designs. Therefore, during one game, Reg borrowed a bat from his team captain which he had just re-stringed and re-spliced for his young son. Consequently, it looked like a tiny autograph bat in Reg's buckets.

As Reg faced his first delivery, with the junior bat, he unsurprisingly lunged and took an almighty swipe at the ball, which went for a six, followed by the blade of the bat, attached to the unravelling string from around the handle that he was still holding. As he walked off to ask reluctant team members for a replacement, the captain couldn't believe that Reg had destroyed his son's newly refurbished bat in one fell swoop, "Look what you've done to my son's bat you ham-fisted oaf!" he said almost in tears.

"Sorry about that, skipper. You'll need to take that back and complain about the poor standard of workmanship."

"No, I'll need to apologise for my poor choice of friends."

"It could have been worse."

"How?"

"It could have been my bat," said Reg.

It's a wonder that Reg had any friends. Even his darts partner Wally Hyde put up with a great deal of irritation and buffoonery, being the butt of Reg's jokes "I said he was named Wally Hyde because he couldn't throw a straight dart." (*Wally-eyed*)

"Really?" was my reply in a kind of weary and exasperated way.

"No, not really," was his reply in both an irritating and humorous, not to mention predictable way.

It wasn't the only time Wally had received little sympathy from Reg. Wally told him that he had to go to the hospital to have his toes removed because of his diabetes. Reg told him not to worry because his operation could be quite beneficial to him, "How in the name of God could this be beneficial to me?" said Wally aghast.

"Well, you'll be able to stand closer to the bar. You won't have to cut your toenails ever again, and I take the same size feet, so I'll buy your slippers."

Wally looked at his questionable 'friend' in a manner revealing his disbelief, but even if Reg had interpreted Wally's facial expression to mean what he had intended, it mattered not because Reg was on a roll, "Oh, and another thing Wally, you won't be able to refer to it as a 'foot' anymore because it will only be eleven inches long."

# Chapter Twenty-Three

Reg enjoyed working for Hunting Surveys as a packer/odd job man and driver between 1975 and 1988. In his own words—"It was the best job I ever had," and he took it seriously, receiving much credit for his reliability and hard work. However, when the company was downscaled and relocated, Reg was made redundant. It was an unhappy time for him. He managed to secure similar work with the company that took over the site, but it wasn't long before they went into administration and Reg found himself in the same position.

He tried to find employment, but it was difficult for a man in his late fifties to secure anything, much less something he enjoyed. So, Ruth suggested he should go back to doing what he was originally trained to do—landscaping and gardening. She even agreed to help him with the workload; something he has never forgotten—"Without her help, I don't think I could have managed."

He slowly built up his business and soon gained a reputation for his high standard of workmanship.

Some of the gardens he took on posed a huge challenge, but he always invoked his time-honoured mantra, "Upgrade the lawn and half the job is done." It was true that when the lawn was cut with a roller to achieve those clean lines, depressions levelled, then edged and treated, the overall effect was to bring the garden in question back to an acceptable standard. Then he would set about weeding the borders and turning the soil, to raise the profile of the shrubs and bedding plants. Overgrown hedges and trees would be sensitively shaped, by removing inward-growing branches or boughs at the right time of year, to reflect their natural shapes or remove dead or diseased wood.

Back in the seventies, I learnt a great deal from Dad that I in turn passed on to my children.

Some of his phrases were memorable as he taught us how to lay lawns… the hard way! The principles were the same, whether using 'elbow grease', 'Heal-and-toe footslogging', 'double-digging', or 'wide-wooden-rake handwork'. We wouldn't dream of using such labour-intensive methods today on large gardens. Reg would even make his own tools; large, heavy and sometimes cumbersome but effectual.

After exhausting preparatory work, the turf was bedded correctly, by which I mean lengthwise on borders and overlapping like brickwork laterally, Dad would say… "Right, time for the persuader now, son."

His 'persuader' was a homemade hand punner or tamper for helping the grassroots to knit into the soil. It comprised a two-and-a-half-foot wide (75 cm in today's money) section of hand-sawn log, approximately four inches (10 cm) thick, morticed and screwed into a long handle. It weighed a ton and got progressively heavier—or appeared to do so—with every successive up-and-down movement by the user. It effectively thumped the turf root system into the soil, with concussive force.

Then everything became a 'persuader' by request when force was inevitably required... mallet, hammer, sledgehammer to get a root or stone out of the ground. Rather like an episode of Top Gear, when Jeremy is trying to carry out or 'doing mechanicking'.

Back in the seventies, there was no industrial plant that was affordable or easily accessible like today. Reg had muscles like Popeye and would work with so much energy until he became pop-eyed and bathed in a pool of his own sweat. He could sweat for England. I do believe this intense physical work over the years has kept him so fit, unlike the time when we were infants, he attempted to saw up some logs in the back garden. He enjoyed a smoke back then, but never in front of us, as he never wished us to adopt the habit.

When he came back indoors in much the same condition as I remember him in at the end of a long working day, Ruth asked him if he had finished sawing all the wood, "You've got to be joking," came the reply. "I've barely got through the first log."

The experience frightened him and from that moment he gave up cigarettes and never touched another one; arguably, one of the best decisions of his life!

Reg was a grafter in the true sense of the word, and we've all admired his dedication to providing for his family. Any monies he gained throughout his working life were *all* given to Ruth and any spending money he required came from her. We never went without. They both put the needs of the family first.

How many men do you imagine would do this today? Ours was in every sense of the word a matriarchal family, in which we all felt secure and loved. However, discipline was never overlooked and with a family of seven in a three-bedroomed, semi-detached house, it was necessary.

Every single day, we children always went to school in clean clothes, until we were old enough to look after ourselves. We wanted for nothing when our parents saw potential in our interests and skills. Any additional requirements were paid for, with income from overtime at work.

Before I became a head teacher, I worked in a mobile soft drinks and grocery business. Ruth packed potatoes in five and ten-pound bags in all types of weather. She often worked in the back garden in sub-zero temperatures or driving rain. This was made slightly easier by the makeshift shelter that Reg built. She wore fingerless gloves and woolly hats to keep warm in the winter months. Her workspace probably resembled a scene from *Steptoe and Son*, but it was certainly an illustration of her unwavering support.

Molly also was a caring grandmother and loaned me fifty-two pounds (a fortune in the seventies) so that I could purchase an initial, cheaply made Chinese euphonium, to enable me to play in the school orchestra and eventually the local brass band, in which I played for twenty-one years, with upgrades of instruments when I could afford them.

Molly died of a heart attack whilst I was in my second year of teacher-training on a trolley in a corridor in Watford General Hospital; an ignominious end to a life that might have been saved by accessible technology, but also a sad indictment of a struggling NHS. There is little change with the stresses that COVID-19 and all its variants have put on our front-line medical teams today. The NHS saved my life after suffering a heart attack in 2015 and I have nothing but praise and heartfelt thanks for the doctors and angels assigned. The latter certainly deserve more recognition for their dedication and at times, unappealing work.

After my attack, which featured some unexpected but amusing incidents (these are covered in another publication) it was a while before specialists could properly calibrate the right doses within the cocktail of drugs prescribed to me. Consequently, I passed out twice, once at the top of our stairs whilst Reg and Ruth were visiting. I know this caused my elderly parents much distress and concern and when I came to on one occasion, I could hear Dad say in a tearful voice... 'It's not right, children should never go before their parents'.

I was fifty-seven! Fast forward to today and they are still more concerned about how we siblings are, rather than worry about themselves; even if their heating or electricity has gone down or have suffered a ceiling collapse from a burst pipe, which occurred months previously. Although they had insurance, they had not made a claim for any repair work, to avoid... 'causing anyone any bother'!

When I eventually discovered this damage, it was after Reg had experienced a fall and had literally split the palm of his hand and had been bandaged like a boxer. He was in a great deal of pain when I called out the assessor, who in turn sanctioned the highest settlement because in his words he 'felt sorry' for Reg. Like so many people of their age, who had witnessed terrible events as children, such as 'The Blitz', 'Doodlebugs' and V2 rockets, there was no deception, just a reluctance to *make a fuss*!

Between the ages of four and five, Ruth's *parents* (Grandparents) moved from the Isle of Wight to Highbury in 1937; not a visionary move by Wallace Herman Hart and his wife Phoebe. On reflection, they should have kept up with events in Europe because they found themselves in a ring-side seat when the war kicked off!

As a schoolteacher, I have found their primary source of evidence about the war fascinating and have even invited them into the classroom to share their sometimes frightening but informative experiences. For example, Ruth lived on Loraine Road off Holloway Road in London throughout the Blitz as a seven-year-old before *moving a short distance* to a larger *top flat* in Caledonian Road! As bombs rained down night after night, her only protection from potential life-threatening blasts, was to take shelter under the kitchen table or bed.

Whilst in the flat, the next threat came from 'Doodlebugs'(V1s) and V2 rockets. During this time, she would take refuge with her Great Aunt May in the bottom flat, along with other residents who lived on the higher floors in the tenement. On one day, she remembers hearing the banshee wailing of the sirens *twenty-three* times!

She remembers at this tender age, lying with Great Aunt May in bed when a mighty blast shocked her out of sleep and made her leap over the bottom of the bed, swearing 'Bloody hell!' as she did so. This according to Ruth, greatly shocked May more than the explosion of a detonating V1!

She vividly recalls a Luftwaffe incendiary device landing in front of their building and one of the worried residents coming back inside to raise the alarm, "Well, put it out with the sand bucket, before it burns the place down," said a precocious Ruth.

She occasionally evokes the sad and ironic memory of a family on her road getting killed by a bomb blast, as they left their house to seek refuge in a street shelter. The shelter got a direct hit. Reg tells a similar story of a family who lived nearby, who would have survived had they ignored the directive to leave their house.

Reg said he was out walking with his mum on one occasion when they heard the definitive tearing and rasping sound of a V1 or 'doodlebug' overhead. Then its engine suddenly cut out as it reached its predetermined distance. As the advice of the time suggested, they ran towards it so that it might glide over them. Instead, it immediately dropped like a stone into a nearby field, whereupon it detonated; the subsequent blast hurling a cow over their heads! My immediate reaction to this astonishing event was to ask Reg how he and his mother felt at the time. I should have known better than to set him up for a typical dead-pan response, "It was really frightening and dangerous son; the 'steaks' were high."

Ruth, not before time, was eventually evacuated to Gypsy Lane in Exmouth at the end of '43/'44; in itself, an ordeal for a young girl, but how she was not sent away during 'Operation Pied Piper' years before is a complete mystery. Molly and her relatives must have thought that they would face the threats and uncertainty together as a family. They weren't alone:

*The Times* newspaper reported on the finding of a wartime diary belonging to Private Kenneth Hawkins who died on 10th September 1943 at Salerno. He records the loss of friends, lack of sleep affecting the 'nerves' and near escapes from the enemy. As his unit sailed up the coast to the landing site, they were bombarded by coastal guns and air attack.

Within the context of today's heightened awareness of mental health issues, I fully recognise the genuine severity of certain cases and the suffering of individuals and their families. I have witnessed the effects of and have lost staff and parents to this deadly unseen illness, though I can't help but think that those especially serving in the emergency or armed forces or having lived through the horrors of two World Wars must have had or possess a higher threshold of tolerance.

I cannot begin to comprehend the depths of suffering or depression that lead people with mental health problems to take their own lives, though I feel anger rise in me when I hear people use casual references to this condition on media platforms because they've sustained the 'hardships' of a 'lockdown', or had to revise for an interview or exam.

Jewish employers of a similar age would share their disturbing accounts to Reg and Ruth, of family members being rounded up by the Nazis and never being seen again. Similarly, we have heard the accounts of surviving members of the Somme, the Battle of Britain, the Battle of the Atlantic or D-Day. How so many of these got through their terrible ordeals to live a 'normal life' is simply baffling.

I've promised myself a visit to Gypsy Lane, Exmouth and nearby Slapton Sands sometime whilst tackling the South-West coastal walk, to pay my respects to those soldiers who died on an exercise prior to D-Day and try to imagine a young girl not so far away, thinking of her family so far away.

# Chapter Twenty-Four

Ruth and Reg have been married for seventy-one years! (June 2024) I asked Reg… What is a seventieth wedding anniversary called? He said, "A long-time son!"

"A bloody long-time son!" said Ruth correcting Reg, thus inviting a look of perplexion from him.

"Florence Nightingale was exceptionally brave and had to endure some appalling sights and tasks; cleaning up after some filthy, smelly, disgusting and lice-infested war-torn soldiers, but she didn't have to sleep with them." Again, Reg tried to look indignant, but his long record of trench-warfare sanitation rendered this gesture ineffectual.

In 2003, I was driving back home from school one evening, when I suddenly remembered that in three days' time it was to be my parents' fiftieth wedding anniversary. I called Mum, who was looking forward to the celebration of this milestone event, at the Elstree Tennis Club where Reg maintained the grounds. My sister Babs and 'Trix' were organising the event.

Finding it difficult to decide what to buy them, I asked Ruth what she would like for a present. In her normal unhelpful way to such requests, she replied that there was nothing they either needed or wanted, "Just your presence will be enough, son." I had two responses to this, both Reg-esque, "Yes, but what *presents* will they be, or am I going to be the only one there?"

"No, really son, let's just have a wonderful time getting together." Then there was a pause, the kind of pause that heralds the truthful answer, "Well, there is one thing that your dad and I would like…"

"And what's that?" I enquired.

"Well, we'd like you to write us a song, son."

"A song? (That was a curve-ball) but I've only got three days to write it!"

Then came the undisguised attempt at reverse psychology, "Well, if you don't think you could manage it, don't worry about it, son."

"It's not that I don't think I could manage it, it's just that I've only got three days to complete it."

I heard her call to Reg… "He says he can't do it because he's only got three days."

"Well, he should have rung earlier and that would have given him more time."

"All right, all right, I'll see what I can come up with, bye."

I was immediately confronted with two problems: Firstly, how was I going to come up with the music and lyrics in such a short timescale and secondly, how does one come up with a romantic song involving fishing and darts?

After much racking of one's mind, I decided that it might be a good idea, to write a waltz. In this way, I would only have to think about the music and not have to worry about writing lyrics involving 'three in a bed' or roach-poles. They would also be able to dance to a waltz in their honour, whilst other guests looked on and feted their achievement.

So, with a three-beats-to-the-bar time signature, I started tapping out a rhythm on the steering wheel. Then as if by divine intervention, a repetitive 'ear-worm' phrase came into my head, "Will you come back... will you come back, will you come back... and love me again."

By the time I arrived home, I had a substantial amount of the first and second verses completed, and by the end of that evening, the song was almost completed. Amazingly, the 'middle-eight' even contained passable references to their hobbies. I spent the rest of that night working out an accompaniment on the guitar and called my harmonica-playing friend Bert who lived in Norfolk, to ask for assistance. He agreed to come to the event at very short notice, and we put him up.

Our first and only rehearsal took place at the event, not long before Reg and Ruth were invited to take the floor. Incredibly, with just the two instruments and my vocals, the song not only sounded half decent but appropriate. Ruth found the music and lyrics overwhelming and shed a tear. Reg didn't hear the words or pay much attention to the music... he was too busy trying not to step on his wife's toes!

In fairness, the song is one of the best I've penned and to this day Ruth admits that it always makes her cry when she hears it. I too find it hard to fight back the tears of emotion.

I'm having to entrust this song to my son and nephew George as I don't want it lost in perpetuity. You never know, if Ed Sheeran reads this, he might consider it worthy of a collaboration.

# Will You Come Back and Love Me Again?

Will you come back and love me again?
Will you bring back the memories of when
Both you and I had the stars in our eyes
Will you come back and love me again

Will you come back and take me away
To the places where you and I stayed?
Wine, passion, flowers, those intimate hours
Will you come and love me again?

Casting our dreams on the fast-flowing streams
Feeding the swim of our love
Finding the double of two single minds
Will you come back and love me again

Will you come back and relive the years?
Will you bring back the laughter and tears?
Spring in our hair and the seasons to share
Will you come back and love me again?

Obviously, Ruth said 'No!'

# Chapter Twenty-Five

For many years, Reg has enjoyed cooking, and this isn't because Ruth can't or won't cook. On the contrary, Ruth has won prizes for her much sought-after apple pie or Victoria sponge. Her nephews and niece can't get enough of them. Her pickled onions are extraordinary too.

My son adores them. Like Reg, he loads himself up with these, like a cowboy might fill his Winchester rifle with shells. The rapid explosive discharges are the same! I always ask my mother to make me a jar every Christmas, though despite efforts to tempt my wife, I can't entice Gwynneth to partake. She says, "It's the smell of them," but I'm not sure if that's before or after their consumption. After witnessing the effects of these on others, I presume she doesn't want her silk underwear to end up looking like Nottingham lace or the indicator ribbons on air-conditioning units!

Despite Ruth's baking and pickling achievements, there was one dish in particular that she made when we were kids, that didn't go down too well and that was steamed roly-poly. The concept sounds tasty and inviting, with bacon and onions wrapped in suet pastry. However, I'm sure it would have been better received, had the onions been caramelized and the bacon partially cooked, prior to being rolled up in the flour and fat and put in the steamer. My memories of this culinary disaster are of the raw meat and onions being steamed to a state of limp tastelessness within a well-cooked casing.

In fairness, this is the only negative example of her endeavours that I recall. To this day I try very hard to emulate her wondrous 'Canary' or syrup pudding and get close enough by religiously following her *Good Housekeeping* cookery book recipe.

Both Ruth and Reg must have worked hard to provide for five teenagers at a time when a higher percentage of income went on food shopping bills. My son's appetite alone threatened to force me into applying for a shelf-stacking job at Tesco, working nights! He went through our cupboards like 'Pac-Man', munching every consumable in sight. He could down a tin of preserved delights faster than 'Popeye' could make spinach disappear and all before and after any meal was dished up.

As a teenager, I distinctly remember arriving home from school one afternoon, to see Reg preparing something for tea. In excited anticipation, I asked him what culinary delight he had in store for us, "Bread and dripping, son."

"*Bread and dripping?*" I replied in muted tones. I thought this rumoured 'meal' was suffered by starving northerners because nothing else was available to them. I had even heard that that publicans in Yorkshire gave it away free on Sundays to passing families, who couldn't afford both food and drink!

My overwhelming sense of disappointment must have instantly registered with Reg's innate anti-ingratitude response mode.

"You ungrateful sod! It was good enough for us to eat during the war."

"Yes, I'm sure it was," I replied… "but I want what you fought for, not what you fought on!"

Reg didn't know whether to admonish my temerity or applaud my wit. After revealing a poorly disguised smile, it fell to the former.

Ruth never learnt how to drive, so it's always fallen to Reg to drive to the local supermarket in the town centre of Borehamwood—which they still rather charmingly refer to as 'the village', to purchase their day-to-day requirements. In their youth, it probably was a village, but now it is a sprawling commuter town, with more and more townhouses springing up like Japanese 'knotweed'. When I came to visit Mum and Dad more recently, I ended up getting lost driving through my *place of birth*! It should be called 'Hometown' now… it's full of homes!

I have often suggested to Ruth that she might consider learning to drive, "What, at my age?"

"Look, it's never too late," I replied once, "What, to kill someone?" A fair comment I thought.

On one occasion, Reg told Ruth that he was going to the shops to get some 'thick chips'(chunky-chips), to which she replied that she would make a list of a few extra things required. Reg then asked her to put the thick chips down on the list so that he wouldn't forget.

It's true and quite understandable that Reg's eyesight now is not what it used to be. In fairness, without spectacles, he couldn't spot a barn along with its door, flown in by a Chinook helicopter. He once took to borrowing a pair of binoculars that Ruth had won in a fishing competition to watch the fortunes of other anglers. To be fair, there was more chance of his charm bringing people closer.

Having erroneously left his glasses in the car, he sought the help of an assistant to find the listed groceries. She was very generous as she was patient with her time and ended up helping Reg to find all the listed items except for one, "I don't think we do 'Brainless chips' sir."

"Brainless chips? Brainless... No, that's my wife's idea of a joke love. I want some thick chips."

"Ah, a bit of a wit then your wife, eh?"

"Oh yes, definitely. A cryptic crossword clue might suggest I invite a foolish sort to tea... get it? 'Twit'!" Years of solving crossword puzzles have certainly helped to upgrade his insults.

Quite recently, Reg was in his local supermarket approaching the express counter with a 'vertically challenged' individual in front. There was a checkout till on either side of the counter and Reg leaned forward to ask which side the man was going. Without reason, the man suddenly replied acerbically and mumbled a withering cascade of abuse, "Alright Grumpy, keep your hair on! (Obviously, he was also follically challenged.) I'm only trying to be polite."

Reg was still filling his carrier with goods as the individual passed by him, and he couldn't resist one more verbal swipe, "And when you get back home, Grumpy, I hope Snow White and the other dwarfs give you a damn good hiding."

Reg then turned to the checkout attendant, struggling like others to hide her laughter and said, "I got that one off Billy Connolly, but it's amazing what you can get away with when you're ninety. What are aggressive people going to do... threaten to kill me?"

Reg's intransigence towards foreign food during my formative years was not uncommon in people of his generation. "I don't want any of that foreign muck," he would say with predictable regularity. His revulsion for takeaway food was and is, every bit as intense, if not as extreme as his abhorrence of 'Beatles' music which, despite our concerted efforts to change, has remained resolute. I'm not convinced his repugnance of either has come about through painstaking research, but more likely through a personal, unswerving opinion, formulated by crystallized tastes and lack of exposure to innovation.

Nevertheless, one of his gardening employers, a Hindu was kind enough to invite him and Ruth to the third day of his daughter's wedding celebrations. Their official invitation, written in red ink and adorned with an image of Ganesha the elephant god arrived in the post.

I don't think Reg or Ruth for that matter, had any idea of the length of celebrations linked to this kind of colourful and splendid event, with its many rituals and mini ceremonies; not to mention the vast amounts of food.

When they arrived early in the morning at the venue, the celebrations were taking place on various floors. After removing their shoes before entering the hall where the wedding was taking place, Reg was surprised at the huge array of footwear left outside. What was more surprising to him was the length of time he was required to sit on his backside with his legs crossed. Occasionally, he would remove himself to go to the toilet or avail himself of the food supplied.

Of the most obvious things that one shouldn't do at a Hindu wedding, or any wedding for that matter, is to wear inappropriate clothing or talk through the wedding ceremony itself. Whilst observing these fundamental requirements, Reg didn't fulfil an additional unlisted rule which states that other people's shoes should not be thoroughly mixed up and laces tied together, when bored. This symbolic act of bringing people together was Reg's parting gift, and he didn't stay long enough to witness the very large congregation's unappreciative response.

I'm sure it wouldn't have taken Chief Superintendent Foyle of the Hastings police, to fathom out who was behind this wilful act of disturbance, but suffice it to say, had Western doctrine decreed that guests remove footwear at my wedding, he would have done the same there. For heaven's sake, he did it at my golf club… twice! However, one surprising point of interest is that he enjoyed some of the Indian food. So not a complete 'bootless errand' or unprofitable venture.

One further reference to the eating habits of my father is his easy-to-please attitude when it comes to cooking. There is very little that he will turn his nose up at, even to the point of enjoying Ruth's roly-poly. He'll wade through the delights of offal; be it liver, kidneys, heart or tripe, and this predilection for the cheap end of butchery has been handed down to his children. Despite our school cooks engaging in the practice of metamorphosis, or alchemy by miraculously turning liver (well it does contain iron) into green saddle ware, we've learnt how to flash-fry it properly.

We also have passed down the economics of slow-cooking cheap cuts of meat, that others might turn down or inexplicably throw away. I once gave a cookery lesson to parents at my school, revealing how they could prepare a Christmas dinner for four at less than £5.00. I used a large turkey leg costing £2.99 and slow-roasted it for five hours... delicious!

However, it's worth noting that the pandemic lockdown has prompted the younger generations to discover how offal and animal appendages have become a cheap source of rich flavour and nutrition. These adventurous 'carnisplorers' are beginning to appreciate more sustainable nose to tail eating; not to mention the vast savings to be made.

My son could easily endure the delights of a bush-tucker trial in... "I want to be a celebrity, get me over there," whereas my daughter and son-in-law still haven't grasped the subtle differences between 'use by' and 'best before' dates.

Having said all this, there is one dressing that Reg cannot abide and that is mayonnaise. One taste of it without doubt and quite extraordinarily, will aggressively activate his gag reflex.

The truth is that it's found across a wide range of food products and is sometimes quite hard to avoid. We have sat with Reg on many occasions when he has given the waiter or waitress a food order and distinctly requested in his endearing way that it not contain 'That muck!' only to bite into it and almost throw up after tasting the 'Devil's condiment'. This result might appear comical to the onlooker if it had not been for the fact that some poor souls have *died* or very nearly, as a result of the ineptitude of workers in some food outlets.

Luckily, laws governing food processing are more thorough these days. I know that allergic reactions from the consumption of certain foods, such as 'anaphylaxis' from peanut products, were a constant worry during my time as a head teacher. On more than one occasion, I suffered the anxiety associated with the administration of 'EpiPens'.

Reg has never adopted airs or graces when dining out, so the decision to invite him to accompany a large party of us to 'Simpsons' in the Strand to celebrate my twenty-first birthday, promised to provide all sorts of entertainment. We did enjoy his company, even though he purposely summoned one of the waiters with all the flair and finesse of an East End docker, by referring to him as 'Chief' whilst requesting a pint of beer. Now, I can appreciate—to some extent—how someone with that level of experience, in that time old, honoured tradition within an archaic setting, where accepted behaviour and etiquette reign, might take umbrage or just a smidgen of resentment.

Nonetheless, this waiter revealed a level of pomposity which rendered it impossible for any of us to endure or support his cause: "I think sir is mistaking me for the wine waiter. I'm the cutlery waiter."

"Oh, I am so dreadfully sorry. (Oh dear! The over-the-top apology heralded a rude comeback, and I wasn't quick enough to intercept it.)"

"Well, do you think you might find the wine waiter and prod him in the arse with one of your silver service forks and ask him to bring me a pint of beer... please."

He turned to me and ironically reminded me how important it was to be polite to others by always saying 'please' when requesting something. "Never forget that, son."

"I won't, Dad, and thanks for the advice."

The beer never came, but to this day, despite my father's lack of articulate or social intercourse, I can only conclude that in not carrying out Reg's request, the waiter not only revealed a lack of professionalism but took snobbery and pomposity to another risible level.

# Chapter Twenty-Six

Skiing is not everyone's cup of tea as it were and as youngsters, we were brought up to regard it as a sport for the privileged and wealthy. Therefore, it was not until I was forty that I had my introduction to it. So, not with a little trepidation, we agreed to accompany my sister and brother-in-law, along with their three very young boys to Zell Am See in the Austrian Alps during the winter of 2002.

Gwynneth could in fact ski, but I was to the sport like Sumo wrestlers were to figure skating.

Naturally, my parents were along for the views and babysitting duties.

"At our age, we're already on the slippery slope," Reg confided. For that reason, they had no interest in participating in 'downhill disasters'.

So, all eleven of us (including our daughter Laura 11 and Harry 4) loaded up a minibus borrowed by my brother-in-law and set off on the monotonous, tiring and gruelling journey to this winter wonderland like the 'Clampits' in the American sixties sitcom 'The Beverly Hillbillies'. Clearly, travel by aircraft was still regarded as a reserved method of transportation for the rich and privileged, or just an expensive alternative.

After what seemed a twenty-four-hour version of 'Le Mans' for vans, with long bouts of travelling, regular changes of drivers and continuous sleep deprivation, we emerged wearily from our entombment and unfurled our limbs at the picturesque destination. And to be fair, it was beautiful. The snow-capped mountains gleamed and glowed in the weakening afternoon sunlight. Everywhere looked fresh, crisp and clean, apart from the inside of our minibus, which looked and smelled like the inside of a badger's set.

Ruth had always expressed a wish to go to Austria—albeit bound up in a kindergarten experience—but the cultural delights as well as the breathtaking scenery were not disappointing.

For the sake of some company, I asked Reg if he would be game for a lesson or two. "Son, I don't know if you've noticed, but it's bloody slippery out there. Looking at some of those 'Kamikaze' characters up there, it looks like they are tied to the front of an out-of-control Exocet missile. The closest you'll get me to it is watching 'Pingu'."

"I'd have to be 'piste' wouldn't I?"

Oh, I wondered when that pun was forthcoming.

After settling into our accommodation, the next task involved getting measured and kitted out for the up-and-coming 'ordeal'. As it was change-over day, there was a queue of people and children waiting to be serviced. This was also Christmas time. One useful tip... Never go skiing at Christmas time or more specifically, at *half-term*, unless you love the notion of waiting or being upstaged by foreign infants whizzing around you like bullets in a crossfire, with tabards that make them look like industrious 'Minions'.

All I can say with some conviction is that I looked good in my outfit, despite feeling like a Mafia victim, encased in a concrete overcoat, supporting a motorway bridge! At least the food in the hotel that night was worth looking forward to.

The next morning, we all had to get the bus to the cable car to take us up to the glacier. To say it was crowded is to fall helplessly short of the fact. Experienced, intermediate, beginners, show-boaters and outright posers, all jostled and shuffled together, like fusing atoms in a 'CERN' particle physics accelerator. Despite the ascending steam bath ritual, the views at the top were both memorable and remarkable.

Once at the base of the ski-lift, my brother-in-law and sister decided to extract themselves from the group, along with Gwynneth, to carry out a *'reconnaissance'* or orientation of the area... and that's when the 'fun' ensued; not least of all, because they didn't come back!

Having spent some time with Harry and Laura, playing in the snow, I left the former in the company of the latter to be overseen by Reg, whilst I spent a short while optimising the time waiting for our 'long-range desert force' to report back. Clicking my enormous size twelve boots onto the skis, I 'slip-slid' away to find the nearest slope. I didn't take the lift to the top of the slope, least of all because I didn't know how. For goodness' sake, I wasn't *that* stupid! So, I struggled to shuffle my way a short distance up the lower slope, before attempting to ski down.

At this point, it is probably worth noting for any newcomer to the sport, the value of learning first how to stop before setting off downhill. You see there is a symbiotic relationship between newly waxed skis and snow crystals; a mutually beneficial relationship if you will. So, with a sweaty brow and nervous disposition, I prepared to set off... and set off I did!

In not conforming to the rules of nursery-slope conventions, I stood up straight with my weight on the back of the skis which I had placed perfectly parallel to each other. The resulting movement forward I imagine, was akin to that of a drag-race hot-rod off the starting line, achieving nought-to-sixty in two-point-four seconds! Scenery and people alike shot past me as if I was looking out of a 'Bullet-Train' window. Fear had gripped my vocal cords, rendering them inoperable until I flew off the piste, where I collided with a signpost and broke my thumb.

Without apologising for my '*French*' the crisp, cold, quiet, stillness of the mountain air was rent with a barrage of invective. That was it, I made up my mind on the spot that skiing was beyond me and at that moment, of course, it surely was!

With an overwhelming sense of underachievement and hopelessness, I shuffled back to where the rest of the family were. I knew for sure I wouldn't be competing for any winter-Olympic medals soon.

Harry was pleased to see me, so I unclipped the suicidal sliding gear and opted for a sledge. Of course, what I didn't do was change my footwear, mainly because I didn't have an option.

I was therefore resigned to the fact that I had to trudge around with what felt like Lurch's preferred choice of platform shoes, whilst Harry had cute, little fur-lined wellies.

In an instant, he just took off into the milling crowd of multi-international downhill skiers and their snowboarding arch-rivals. I had no chance of catching him up, much less in stopping his absconding. Within seconds of being in full view, he was gone, lost and out of sight.

A shot of adrenalin coursed through my body and all at once, I was gripped with panic and irrepressible fear! I surveyed the mass of indifferent cold-weather revellers. Why didn't they too feel the sense of urgency that had surged over me? How dare they continue pursuing their fun-filled activities when I was feeling so bereft? I had to draw their attention to my plight. There was no time to lose. I wanted to tell them to stop what they were doing. Sort this problem out first and then continue with their merriment.

Now I'm sure at some point, *most* parents have experienced that stomach-churning, gut-wrenching, cold sweat-inducing moment when a youngster has suddenly vanished. Quite often only momentarily, Sometimes, for a few minutes but rarely for fifteen minutes or longer. I had only one recourse of action and that of course was to howl like a wolf or banshee at the top of my voice, "Harry, Harry, HARRYEEEEE!" That got people's attention all right, but the '*bastards*' weren't doing anything about my plea of desperation.

They just carried on about their business, looking at me with indifference, wondering what the disturbance was all about. I continued to wail with all the volume and passion I could muster. Reg came over with the prerequisite amount of concern on his face. "What's the matter, son? What the hell is up?"

"I've lost Harry, he's disappeared into the crowd! Get Mum to look after the kids. Send Laura over to help me. Check in all the bars and restaurants. We've got to find him."

I shouldn't have had enough time to think of blaming Gwynneth for not being there, but I found it, although somewhat fleetingly.

"Stop shouting that loudly, son, you're going to set off an avalanche," cried Reg. I was suddenly aware of my earnest cries reverberating and echoing around the Austrian Alps. Reg was absolutely right. I suppose there was a chance of prompting a geological disaster, so I responded accordingly, "Fuck that, we've got to find him. We're losing the light!"

True enough, the light was fading, the lifts were shutting down and the mass crowd was beginning to thin as they made their way to the descending cable car.

I made my way amongst the baffled, confused, non-responding, departing and depleting snow-lovers. Laura had joined in with my demented caterwauling.

I started off with a plan of action, but soon just wandered at random to all points of the compass, wailing wildly and incessantly to no one and everyone. Laura tried to calm me down because I was worrying her, but I was inconsolable.

Then, after a period of time—approximately a quarter of an hour—which seemed like an eternity, a man approached me, holding the hand of a little boy who looked distinctly like Harry the closer they became. In a strong, Dutch accent, he asked, "Is dit jouw zoon 'arry. Eees dis 'arry?" The man looked like he could have been Harry's father. Had he decided to kidnap him, no one would have thought they were not related. He had pure blond hair and brown eyes, with a naturally pale complexion. I looked down upon a smiling Harry. I could have squeezed the life out of him, held him in my embrace and lovingly kissed him—the Dutchman I mean!

"Oh, thank you, thank you, thank you! Where did you find him?"

"Hij was bij de kabelbaan… de kable-kar."

"What were you doing there, Harry?"

"Trying to find Mummy!"

After thanking his rescuer profoundly, I set off back to where Ruth and Reg were with the other youngsters. They were equally relieved to see the prodigal son.

By now, it was becoming quite dark and not having skied before, my thoughts turned towards contacting the emergency services to report the missing persons. I asked an English-speaking operative at the cable car, who advised me not to panic as the others would have already found themselves down the mountain. Reticently, we all clambered aboard the cable car and wearily returned to the hotel.

We had been back sometime when Claire, Giles and Gwynneth arrived. They had got to the top of the ski-lift descended the other side and without a piste-map had got hopelessly lost; eventually skiing to the base of the mountain and having to catch a bus back. Having completed a Mountain-Leadership Training Board course in the mid-nineties, I wondered how much ascending a mountain with a map whilst skiing, was similar to a 'day one' requirement in hill or mountain climbing.

After changing, bandaging my thumb, eating and finally getting the kids to bed. We started—by which I mean me—to unwind. Giles said that he would take me to the slope the next day and give me my first lesson. What could possibly go wrong?

The next morning, strongly reminiscent of 'Groundhog Day' we once again suffered the trauma of the early 'push for the summit'. Once again, whilst Reg and Ruth remained with the children (Harry and Laura were both in ski school) Giles said he would take me to the top of a 'blue run' rather than the nursery or 'green' slope and of course therein lay the first mistake of my lesson.

To get to the top of the 'blue' I had to negotiate the infamous and perpetually moving 'T'-bar lift. Ironically, and erroneously, when one first looks upon this contraption, one is inclined to *sit* on the two-person mechanism, rather than correctly stand and allow it to pull against the back of one's legs, whilst holding poles in one hand and grasping the upright, spring-ended stanchion. To have been briefed more precisely would have probably still not helped, because as one makes initial contact with the bar, there is a slight delay and then suddenly the unsuspecting passenger is thrust violently forward and a plough-shape manoeuvre is required with the skis to slow down the 'take-off'.

Having not been shown how to form a plough movement meant this procedure was never engaged. I fell off *three* times. A disillusioned and somewhat embarrassed (I suspect) Giles then said the same as any caring, concerned and helpful instructor would have done in my ear, "If you do that again, I'm off!"

This time, with the threat of failing once again, I clutched the next arriving pole with both hands and exerting all my strength, was transported up the slope like an unfortunate cowboy tied behind and dragged by a galloping horse! That was the easy part. Getting back down proved a little more difficult. Despite Giles's guidance and encouraging manner, these extensions to my feet had a will of their own. I lost count of the times I fell over, luckily into relatively deep fresh powder, but eventually, I did get back down, such was my desire to succeed at this alien sport.

Now at this juncture, not wishing to berate the assistance that I was receiving from my 'instructor', I was nonetheless reminded of how important and relevant my teacher training was, relative to introducing a novice to and explaining the rudiments of a new concept.

I was forever reminding staff at school how professionalism in teacher training often becomes second nature and is perfectly illustrated by struggling guests coming into assemblies or classes and addressing children without the obvious and crucial skills which we took for granted.

Suffice it to say, the following year, Gwynneth, I and the kids went to Bulgaria and received superb and proper instruction from an ex-Olympic skier by the name of Maria. Oh, my days, this elderly and stylish woman was incredible and after only five days, I was jumping, turning and performing parallel stops. We had such a wonderful time which cemented my love of the sport, despite having to travel there and back aboard a rainbow-coloured Russian-built 'Tupolev' aircraft which looked like it belonged to Austin Powers' personal fleet!

The threadbare and basic interior of this ill-designed aircraft, with its unsettling and howling engines, wasn't the worst part of the trip. The on-board refreshments reflected those of a Russian Gulag by which I mean fatty salami in cheap doughy bread followed by a Mars Bar and flushed down with a healthy glass of water. The four-hour flight aboard this condemned and 'Flintstone'-like mode of transport was at best uncomfortable, not to say worrying but coming into land at Manchester was interminable and intolerable. We were stacked for what seemed to be an age, with the engines screaming at every turn of approach.

Just glancing across at the cabin crew's expressions seemed to endorse my worst fears. I genuinely thought this flight was to be our last. When the tyres and engines eventually screeched in a tortured fashion upon landing, my first inclination was to kiss the pilot and wish the crew well on their journey back.

If the outward journey to Austria aboard the 'Minibus Express' was interminable, then the trip back was much worse. We had to endure some extreme and treacherous weather conditions, involving blizzards, along with a fine that we picked up from the Swiss authorities because Giles had overlooked the country's requirement to purchase a road pass!

You live and learn, quite often the hard way!

Within the confined and fetid environment of the minibus, other obstacles to overcome were the loud and lingering effects of Reg's love of sauerkraut; a culinary delicacy and joy that he had been reunited with from his service days in Germany… unbelievable!

# Chapter Twenty-Seven

One memorable and celebratory event which occurred in 2004 was Ruth's winning of her angling club's 'Challenge Cup' trophy. This coveted prize was awarded for the highest combined total of points in *all* competitions for the year, involving lake, river, float and leger fishing.

All the more remarkable was being the only woman to ever achieve this *and* when she was seventy years old! She didn't like using a roach pole because, in certain weather conditions, it became an effective electrical conductor and was also long enough to touch live overhead cables. Indeed, one visiting angler using such a rod, managed to light himself up like a Christmas tree and 'cooked his goose' at the same time. He was partially cremated before they eventually buried him!

Inevitably, when I accompanied my parents fishing and even when she won a preferable seat closer to the entrance in competitions, Ruth always insisted on walking to the furthest swim at the top end of the lake. This of course involved a long, difficult and cumbersome walk with all the bulky equipment. This was bad enough when Reg had my assistance, or rather forced labour, though how he managed on his own is beyond me.

Ruth would load him up like a Himalayan Sherpa's donkey and by the time he had reached the desired spot, would look more like an animal on a R.S.P.C.A. appeal advert!

Upon his exhausted arrival on one such occasion, Reg was upset to discover he had lost his British Darts Organization (B.D.O.) pendant that we kids had bought him for his fiftieth birthday. He did very little fishing that day, but rather incurred unpleasant stinging rashes over his arms, whilst rummaging through nettles attempting to locate it. He was terribly dismayed as it had great sentimental value and asked numerous returning anglers to look for it on the path back to the car park.

At the end of the day, after packing up the equipment and returning the fish back to the water, the pair set off on the long trudge back. Ruth said it was a beautiful evening and as they approached the car, the sun shone through the trees and glinted off the pendant in the long grass. Reg hadn't spotted it, and I suspect that was because sweat must have been running off his furrowed brow, into his eyes! He wearily loaded up the car; a task that might have taken half the time had Ruth revealed beforehand, that she had found the jewellery. She revelled in holding back the discovery and Reg loved her for it.

A few months before the world was paralysed by the unexpected pandemic, known as 'COVID-19' which would bring unparalleled disruption and unprecedented constraints, Reg was experiencing familiar setbacks with his vehicle that had broken down... again! He couldn't understand why the 'AA' or 'RAC' hadn't given them an honorary lifetime membership, in much the same way as their fishing club had. Reg always believed that Field Marshall Rommel or 'The

Desert Fox' (commander of the 'Afrika Korps') had more luck getting serviceable parts to his tanks than he did to his cars. So, desperate to get hold of some transportation to take Ruth to a competition in Thame the following day, he asked Barbara and Trix for some help. Of course, Barbara, the ever-loving and accommodating daughter immediately came to the rescue without thinking. Knowing Trix, I thought he might have… thought about it, that is! Nevertheless, they loaned Reg their car!

Setting off the following morning, once again at a time normal people believe to be a rumour spread by insomniacs, they made their way to Oxfordshire. Upon arrival, Ruth was puzzled to see that no other competitors had turned up for the six-hour competition, as they followed signs to the designated parking site—an open field, provided by a benevolent farmer. In fact, only three anglers turned up that day and two of them were Reg and Ruth. And still, they didn't win! The adjudicator's explanation was that August was the height of the holiday season, to which Reg replied, "If no one registered in advance, why hold the competition and anyway, don't some anglers fish during their holidays?"

"Yes, but not all of them have wives as keen as yours."

"What, to drive forty miles and compete with 'Billy-no-mates' over there?"

Ruth said it had been a depressing day—no doubt a portent of what was yet to come. Undoubtedly, the highlight of her outing was when her favourite bird, a noble kingfisher perched on her rod with five or six wriggling small fry in its bill. Ruth was rendered motionless; staring in awe and wonder at this iridescent blue and orange visitor. It moved its head from side to side, peering at her with each eye in turn, as if to say I can catch fish, why can't you? Then as suddenly as it arrived, it flew off to reward its young with the 'catch-of-the-day'; flashing its luminous colours that seemed to change as it flew rapidly over the surface of the water.

## Summer

Glaring reflections
On a silver stream
Waving leaves of innumerable shades
Fluttering wings transparent
Iridescent colours
Crashing waves on a sandy beach
The sweet nose of cuttings
Flowers' perfumes on the breeze
Scent and flowers sent
Warmly received
Sparkling drinks
Sparkling eyes
Love blooming

In Ruth's eyes, nothing could have equalled or compared with the personal display of colour and beauty, that this little fellow had treated her to but by the end of the day, she would yet again be rendered motionless by the surprise of nature.

At long last, even Ruth was ready to leave as her empty keep-net reinforced the paucity of catches. Packing up they stumbled with their heavy gear back to the car.

When they got to the vehicle, it was surrounded and hidden from view by a herd of cows; not unusual as they were in a farmer's field, but the difficulty in attempting to move 'the silly cows' on, merely proved to be yet another inconvenience in what turned out to be an exacting day.

On closer inspection, they appeared to be licking the car with some animated excitement. After some hind-thrashing with a keep-net pole in a wasted effort to move it on, the herd remained resolute in its licking frenzy. Eventually, and not as a result of any persuasion, the cows lost interest and moved on. The farmer then appeared and was quick to allay any fears that our intrepid duo may have had, "Don't worry about the car, everything seems OK."

It was at this point that Ruth and Reg could see the resulting mess that the beleaguered vehicle had been left in. The driver's side wing mirror was broken and hanging by its wires, but more disconcerting was the layer of slime enveloping the paintwork. The cows had literally licked it from top to bottom, "*OK*? Repeated Reg, *OK*? I suppose the wing mirror would be useful in checking whether any passing terrorist has planted some explosive device under the car. And look at the slime!"

True enough, Trix's and Bab's car looked as if it had been attacked with a 'Ghostbusters' plasma inductor' or covered in a slime secretion by 'Edgar the Bug' from 'Men in Black'.

Initial attempts to remove the congealed, rope-like mucus, were hopeless as indeed was the carwash entered on the way home. It was to take a great deal more scrubbing before the dried, wallpaper paste-like consistency of the aqueous, bovine bile was removed. Only then was the scratched paintwork revealed, caused by the abrasive surface of the cows' tongues!

It's suspected that like dogs, cows are attracted to the road salt or minerals thrown up by the motion of the wheels on road surfaces. This knowledge however was irrelevant to Reg or indeed Trix who wondered if his pride and joy had been entered into a stock-car race.

Of course, more sobering is the fact that Ruth and Reg have not been to their lake or river for several years, ever since something more ruthless, frightening and non-discriminatory than mankind's predilection for war, religious or cultural persecution, waged its own conflict on an unsuspecting global population. Though let's not discount the scientific advances made when such a threat encourages creative efforts to solve the problem: 'Necessity is the mother of invention' Plato (Greek philosopher).

COVID-19
Even with
20-20 vision
No-one saw
That coming

# Chapter Twenty-Eight

When he could find the time Reg would take a holiday which was spent following the practice of his occupation (a busman's holiday) and tidy up our garden. When he got it into his mind, or rather when Ruth got it into hers that it needed to be done, he wasted no time in bringing it back to its former glory.

In the earlier days, not long after we had moved into the house they would eventually own, the garden looked a mess. It needed a patio, which at the time was completed in fashionable 'crazy-paving' because my parents couldn't afford to buy paving slabs. Reg spent a week on his knees—only the second time in his life after asking Ruth to marry him—and eventually put two tons of unwanted broken slabs into an acceptable arrangement.

Like any jigsaw puzzle, there were pieces missing near its completion, but Reg managed to find them by scouring the estate in his van and taking them out of skips! He's always taken things out of other peoples' skips and never needed to order one himself because he's never thrown anything away! As a result, he built himself a sod-off-sized shed out of fencing and other discarded wood, to house everything. To this end our garden often looked like a reclamation yard; in other words, full of stuff that other people might need, but not us!

Similarly, when it came to solving the problem of little topsoil, Reg knew where to find some, in a local stretch of woodland at the bottom of our road. This required him to trundle a wheelbarrow and spade some four hundred yards, with young Peter and me (I suppose it looked less suspicious with kids in tow, although that didn't work with the dynamo incident) and dig out some quality leaf-mould soil. After overfilling the barrow, he would then struggle with it all the way back, numerous times and load up the flowerbeds.

I'm sure Alan Titchmarsh would have disapproved and probably us children as well—if we'd known it was wrong, but the rich, fertile soil certainly benefited the plants and Reg's wallet. This 'Hi ho, hi ho, it's off to work we go' venture, certainly reminds me of sunshine-filled days with a younger, fit father, but it also evokes a later, much darker and sinister event, which left me with a lasting and disturbing memory.

Quite often, during my teens, whilst upstairs in my bedroom completing schoolwork, I would look out upon the playing field behind our house and frequently see an elderly gentleman push his wheelbarrow, tools and vegetables some four hundred yards between his allotment and house which was situated off the path at the bottom of our garden. During the innumerous times, he completed this laborious journey, there were odd occasions when some unscrupulous youths would provoke and torment this dear old man. Through the open window, I along with other residents I suspect, could hear the taunts and wondered why this unnecessary behaviour persisted. I knew many of these boys including the 'pack leader' who attended the same school as us and had been involved in several skirmishes with his bullying acquaintances.

Once, in the local newspaper, it was reported that this poor old man's allotment had been vandalised and his crop destroyed—not even stolen; not that this would have been morally any more acceptable, but perhaps preferable to a man who had worked so tirelessly to cultivate his prized vegetables. Although many suspected the individuals involved in this wicked persecution, no prosecutions were made.

Around October/November time of the same year, I was watching television one evening with Ruth and was shocked to hear a loud bang which came from the path behind our garden.

"Some kids are letting off fireworks again," said Ruth.

"No, I don't think so. That sounded more like a shotgun!" I had gone clay-pigeon shooting with my brass band colleague Richard on several occasions and knew the familiar sound of a cartridge being discharged.

I instantly jumped up—to this day I don't know why—and ran up the garden where in the light provided by a lamppost, I was able to scale the fence. I could hear raised voices as I ascended, but nothing prepared me for what I saw on the other side.

Sure enough, the old man was standing on his doorstep holding a discharged shotgun, with one or two youths screaming, accusing him of shooting their accomplice. Laid on the path, up against the fence, was a lad two years younger than myself, who had been shot in the chest.

In an obvious state of shock, his predicament was made all the more pitiful by the muffled cries for his mother.

The old man's eyes were as wide as saucers; he too was in a state of shock, but with the gun still levelled at his shoulder, repeated the phrase "Leave me alone. Leave me alone!"

In an age when there were no mobile phones, time and swift action were even more crucial considerations, "Leave the old man alone and call 999... now! And someone stay with *the lad*. (I used his name) Put it down sir, help is on the way." He didn't but was frozen into the adopted position and repeated the demand... "Leave me alone. Tell them to leave me alone!"

I raced back to the house, rang the services, just in case, and told them how to access the scene. It wasn't straightforward. I then told them where I would be waiting to take them across the green. What seemed like hours was only several minutes before the ambulance crew and police arrived. I witnessed them stabilise the boy and carry him off, whilst the police conducted their questioning.

I wasn't much use over the shooting incident, but I certainly knew what had led up to it. The boy died on the way to the hospital after suffering an agonising wound. A totally avoidable and unnecessary death and as I write this, I fail to hold back the tears when I think of the misguided, inattentive and neglectful parenting that eventually led to this tragedy.

The poor old man spent a short while in prison I understand. I don't know what became of him, but what advantage could be gained anyway with an early release? He had lost his house, allotment, freedom and possibly any sense of justice and what for... because a young, underachieving child, had been denied the fundamental skills of living in a society; devoid of respect and due regard for the feelings, wishes, rights and property of others. Such a waste of both lives and the incident only serves to remind us of the need for more tolerance, education and understanding in this world.

I too suffered the effects of long-term bullying, but the sense of self-preservation, strength and respect instilled in me by my father, ensured that I would prevail against the tide of oppression and mental torment.

Up to the time of securing the position of head teacher, I metaphorically stamped on bullying. I was hard on the bully and protective of the victims, but essentially supportive of both. In twenty-five years of teaching, I knew of only two 'unstable' children who were not responsive to guidance, punishment or pastoral care. These were the unfortunate kinds that inevitably come to experience a regrettable outcome or go on to lead countries as dictators; either way, choosing a direction that leads to the suffering of many other innocent people.

# Chapter Twenty-Nine

During the mid-1990s, I decided to invite my brother-in-law John and Paul to walk the two hundred and seventy-odd miles of the Pennine Way. Reg was working as indeed was my brother Pete, so I invited them to a later stage of the journey, as we had planned to tackle the route on four separate weekly holidays. As it happened, only Pete joined us on the final stage.

About half way into the venture, we stopped at a pub on the last day before getting a train back home. As we made our way to the bar, we couldn't help but notice an incredibly large and distinguished pair of well-worn service boots, that had been left unoccupied on the carpet. I asked Paul what he wanted to drink, and he replied, "I'll have a pint of what that bloke has just had!"

We were still laughing at the joke when the large guy who so obviously could have filled them came out of the toilet. He indeed was a soldier in the British army who had taken leave (presumably of his senses) to complete the Pennine Way in the fastest possible time. This we thought, was the perfect example of a 'glutton-for-punishment', who should have had enough challenges to keep him satisfied at work!

His boots remained the theme of our lengthy conversation until we bid him good luck and goodbye.

Some years later, Paul and John, along with Reg joined me for the completion of the second stage of the 'Coast-To-Coast' walk. The halfway stage of this path intersects the Pennine Way at Keld and that's where Gwynneth, in the later stages of pregnancy with Harry drove us. After dropping us off, we made our way to the famous farm of Doreen Whitehead. Doreen was the accommodation queen of the Pennine and Coast-to-Coast trails.

What she didn't know about places to stay on these routes, wasn't worth knowing. More importantly, her meals were legendary. No one left her table feeling that they could have eaten more, but many left, wishing they had eaten less! It was impossible to refuse any offerings of her baked comfort. They were wonderful!

No word of a lie! As we approached the front door of Doreen's farm, we looked down and on the step were the *same pair* of boots that we had seen at that bar years ago. There was no mistaking the unique look and size of this footwear; perhaps a little more worn and caked in mud, there was no doubt who these belonged to. Paul, John and I gazed at them, speechless and amazed. What were the chances of encountering them again? Reg thought the chances were high as given their size, one should have no difficulty in spotting them from any point of the compass, "I'd love to use these in helping me to lay turf," he said.

As we laughed, the soldier came out of the door and recognised us, "My God," he said. "I remember you a lot!"

"We don't remember you, but we'll never forget those boots!" said Paul.

It was a memorable reunion.

After exchanging recollections and farewells, we entered the premises where Doreen had anticipated our arrival by laying on tea and cake. When I say tea and cake, what I really mean can only be described as a gut-busting banquet of baked delights, prior to dinner! We were hungry and should have paced ourselves knowing full well that a bigger meal was on its way. As we tucked into one feast, Doreen came amongst us with a notebook to take our orders for later.

After showering and preparing for the following day's walk, we all came downstairs where we sat and waited for our food. Then it came... and kept on coming. The portions were outrageously large. Value for money was not an issue, but the likelihood of death by eating was, "I'm not hungry enough yet after all that cake," said Reg.

"Neither are we, but we can't disappoint Doreen who's gone to so much trouble," I replied.

Everything came with pastry, both dinner and dessert. Our dinner comprised traditional meat pie, mashed potatoes and all the trimmings. When one of the pudding choices arrived, Doreen—although knowing what the response might be—asked everyone what they would like on their 'Spotted Dick', in a rather suggestive way. She shouldn't have because recalling a similar incident on the 'Pennine Way' at Hadrian's Wall, Paul said, "Teeth marks," and Reg followed this up with "Lipstick!"

By the time we had forced the last morsels of calorie-enriched delights down, to a person, we were all feeling like the inevitably exploding 'Mr Creosote' from the famous Monty Python sketch. It was precisely at this moment that Doreen came round once more with her notepad, to ask us all what we wanted for breakfast! Whereas it was an 'After-Eight Mint' that provided the catalyst for Mr Creosote's demise, it was undeniably Doreen's pad and pencil that provoked the look of incredulity and fear on our faces. I pleaded, "Doreen, our stomachs are literally jam-packed, we can't think about any more food, however wonderful it is."

"I have to know before you all disappear so that I can prepare it," replied Doreen. "So what do you all want?"

"We will disappear Doreen, but it will be on stretchers!" said Reg. "Come on! Come on!" said Doreen, "Oh, all right, an opened window," said John.

"Blotting paper," said Paul.

"A bedpan," said Reg.

"Dear God!" said Doreen.

Sadly, I don't think Doreen is still with us, but she was a warm, generous and delightful character whom many will always look back on as being a very special lady. She could've satisfied Desperate Dan's ferocious appetite with her own version of a 'cow pie'!

During the week away, I had purposely arranged for Reg to have a separate room at each bed-and-breakfast we stayed at. We knew his infamous snoring and other sound effects would keep us awake. In truth, he felt a little marginalised and dispirited by this arrangement, but no one felt brave enough to endure the surprises that he would inevitably provide, should they end up sharing with him. It's not that the rest of us weren't capable or guilty of indulging in the same anti-social habits as Reg, it's just that he was considerably louder and more disturbing in his execution of them!

Walking with Reg, like Paul, was a joy. Not only was he fit enough to keep up with us but also extremely entertaining.

Like my brother Pete on an earlier walk, he would insist on carving phallic designs on the tracks throughout the journey, with his stave. When asked why, usually by an exasperated John, he would reply that it was to help lost hikers find their way by putting them in the right direction. He said it was good enough for the occupying Roman army to carve them onto the stones in Hadrian's Wall.

John said it didn't make them any less offensive, especially as we were being followed by two other walkers, "Exactly my point, they've remained behind us and not got lost once and anyway, they might not possess a compass," replied Reg.

"You've definitely lost your moral compass," said John.

John's embarrassment increased as the walkers gained on us. As they drew level, much to John's shocked response and horror Reg said, "Has the signposting been helpful boys?"

"Certainly," said one. "You don't get symbols like that on an 'Ordnance Survey Map'."

What I distinctly remember, was having the time to engage with one another. We had time to converse and perhaps more importantly, listen to each other at a time when individuals or '*nomophobes*' were not predisposed to or 'prisoners' of their mobile phones. It's lamentable that so many of us are dependent upon our phones, to the point of being rude or offensive at gatherings when they shouldn't be required; not to mention experiencing a *mild?* state of panic after misplacing them. How sad it is when people must be reminded at theatres, films or religious ceremonies, to switch off their '*demons*' only to forget and embarrass or agitate the entire audience or performers. Would you believe mobile phones went off at two funerals I attended, and for some reason, the ringtones were loud and/or inappropriate?

Rather than choose a calming and comforting classical piece, such as 'Adagio for Strings' or 'Nella Fantasia', inevitably the tracks are either 'Bat out of Hell' or 'Highway to Hell'. Understandably, most loud ringtones come from the mobiles of elderly owners, who have neither the ability to mute or hear them, because of their lack of technical know-how or deteriorating aural dysfunctions!

The last word on this subject can go to Albert Einstein, "I fear the day that technology will surpass our human interaction…"

Anyway, Paul called Reg 'King Tutt' for reasons that are self-explanatory, but he is also affectionately referred to as 'King of the Puns'. He loves wordplay, and I possess one hilarious memory from our walk when he lovingly assisted me in compiling a list of insults describing himself, would you believe it?

> You put the…
> Bust in combustion
> Stink in distinction
> Dick in predictable
> Wind in window
> Arse in sparse
> Turd in sturdy
> Reg in dredge
> Wrecked in correct

Gust in disgusting … *and then with a flourish of genius, my particular favourite:*

Farter in German

For as long as I can remember and even more applicably in his dotage, Reg, as previously illustrated, has always possessed a razor-like wit. His sense of timing and rapid ripostes are legendary amongst family, friends and unwitting acquaintances. Sometimes I feel that he just waits patiently to use a comeback on some unsuspecting victim.

Recently, Ruth's stylist commented to Reg that she had been her hairdresser for forty years, "Just as well love, can you imagine how long her hair would be now if you hadn't been?"

I've never known him to voice any discontent or disenchantment on his lot as it were. He's always taken life as it comes; wading his way through the quagmire of challenges and finding happiness in his ability to make the most of what we've had. A close family has always been his and Ruth's most celebrated achievement.

When, at the tender age of nineteen, I left my family to work away in the Middle East, I knew every one of the 'Magnificent Seven' felt bereft but also understood the value of my going.

Reg ensured that I was sent occasional 'Red Cross' parcels filled with edible delights and priceless messages of love from home. Nothing was asked or expected of me, other than to stay well and return home safely. Upon my return home in 1978, which coincided with my parent's wedding anniversary, I organised a dinner for twelve family members and close friends at a local golf club, where a friend of mine was a chef. I remember the amount I paid for the celebrational meal at the time comprising starters, mains, desserts and drinks—including champagne. The total for the entire party was £84.00.

We all had a marvellous evening and as we left the venue it started to rain quite heavily. I sat in the front of Reg's light-blue Vauxhall Victor Estate with Reg clanking through the gears with the use of his steering column linkage. The vehicle had seen better days, a fact obviously apparent once again I thought, to the person who sold it to him. "Hadn't you better put the wipers on?" I enquired as Reg squinted through the windscreen of reduced visibility.

"They're not mechanical, they're manual," replied Reg.

I was about to question this remark when he wound down the window and operated them with his right hand as he held on to the steering wheel with his left. Frequently, he would remove his grip from the wipers in order to reverse the use of his hands and operate the column gear lever. He repeated this procedure all the way back from Radlett; some five or six miles and with the linkage constantly slipping out of second gear.

"This second-hand gear is a bit of a nuisance son!" Reg commented with a well-timed pun.

When we got home, I noticed the right sleeves of his jacket and dress shirt were soaked through. That didn't seem to bother Reg, instead, with a beaming smile he merely quipped, "What do you think of my armature replacement for the wiper motor? It's good to have you back, son."

"Likewise, Dad, but isn't there a replacement for a village idiot that you could apply for somewhere?"

Ruth piped up before he could reply, "He's tried son, numerous times, but unfortunately, he's under-qualified! That wiper has been out of action for weeks, but your father says it's only a problem when it rains. He says he tries to avoid going out in it."

"The rain son, not the car!"

Before I left for the Middle East, the brakes had failed whilst I was driving the contraption on the A41! I managed to drive it back just using the handbrake. We had no roadside assistance.

Reg said that it could have been worse. "How in all that is holy, could it have been worse?"

"It could have been me!" he replied. Predictable, but nevertheless amusing!

Realising just how desperate matters had become regarding the family's transportation, I now knew that the down deposit for my house was out of the question. Instead, for the first time in their entire lives, Ruth and Reg got a new 'Vauxhall Cavalier'. Needless to say, we kids benefited from it more than they did.

Reg's love of puns inspired the following poem:

# Pun It for the Fun of it

I met my Kiwi greengrocer friend
Victoria Plum
I said
Jaffa nice day?
She said
Well, lime (I'm) not very well currantly (currently)
And I've lost my Blackberry
I said
Why don't you pop out for one of those pod things—an

Apple?
She said
They don't 'peel (appeal) to me
I said
You look cressfallen (crestfallen)
She said
It's because I'm at the point of despear (despair)
I said
You need to orange (arrange) a peach (beach) holiday
She said
I can't my Nana is off-colour
So I said
Give her a fruit punnet
She said
I hadn't thought of that
Cherry-O (cheerio)
I bet she thought
Doesn't the mango (man go) on
By
Lee K. O'nion

When I was in the process of having the anthology 'Most Secret' published which contained this poem, I received a call from the publisher's office asking if I had gained permission from the writer to include it! "What do you mean?"

"Well, it's written by a fellow called Lee something or other."

Left speechless by the youngster's literal shortcomings in written humour, I replied "Oh, that one? Yes, it's by an old greengrocer friend of mine."

"Oh, that's alright then."

# Chapter Thirty

No one had expected it. The news came like the proverbial 'bolt out of the blue'. On one cold, damp, yet sun-dappled Sunday morning in November 2022 my mobile phone rang; the instantly recognisable 'Magnificent Seven' soundtrack, informing me that it was a call from a family member that had priority and wasn't to be ignored. A tear-inducing cry of grief came from Barbara, informing me that John had died suddenly of a heart attack. At first, her delay in getting the words out, had me thinking it was Dad, but the shock was equally impactful.

My first consideration was for poor Angie, who at the time was dealing with the fallout of unexpected grief in the aftermath of paramedic intervention and other standard procedures.

Apparently, John had awoken alongside her in bed, sweating and complaining of chest pains; classic tell-tale signs—I remember them well! Angie informed him that she was going downstairs to make a cup of tea and by the time she had returned, John had suffered a terminal coronary thrombosis.

Given the enormous demands placed on our emergency services, surprisingly the paramedics arrived in minutes. They immediately set about administering cardiopulmonary resuscitation. After what seemed like an extended period, Angie had let out an impassioned appeal for them to cease their fruitless though necessary procedural endeavours, "Stop it; stop it, for God's sake! Can't you see that he's gone?"

As Barbara conveyed the details of the event, it was hard to fight back the futile thoughts of what might have been avoided, had someone been there to help Angie and indeed John in their dire, life-threatening moment of need.

After concluding the call with Babs, I managed to get through to Angie, who was clearly in a state of shock though nevertheless lucid in her conversation. I couldn't help but admire her sense of resilience and stoicism.

Barbara and Pete, as always quick to respond to action when required, were already in transit to Gravesend. (Who couldn't resist the temptation to point out any obvious irony?) I reassured Angie that they wouldn't be long. On their journey, they had both stopped off at Mum and Dad's house to break the news to them face-to-face, rather than try to explain over the telephone, mindful of their possible reactions to shock. I naturally enquired after their responses.

Babs said they were visibly shaken, but nevertheless remained composed if not indomitable. Later, Babs described Dad's behaviour as that of one suffering 'age guilt'. I understood what she had meant, as I recalled his saying... "Children shouldn't go before their parents," after my event.

Following the conversations with Babs and Angie, I suggested to Gwynneth that we go out for a walk to clear our minds and get our heads around this bombshell. We decided to drive to Slaithwaite, for a walk above the town, finishing with a stretch back along the Huddersfield Narrow Canal.

Shortly after parking the car, we made our way through a small turnstile, into a field to start climbing the gradient. Suddenly, there was a cry from a chap at the top of the hill…

"Have you got a phone?"

"Sorry?"

"A phone… mobile?"

"Yes."

"Well, call for an ambulance. There's a man up here who has collapsed, and I can't help him because his dogs are preventing me from getting close to him." I immediately called the emergency services and was put through to an operator. "Is the patient breathing?"

"Unsure, we can't get close enough to check his vital statistics, but he's definitely not moving."

"So, we'll need dog handlers and possibly mountain rescue if the vehicle can't get close enough."

"Yes, I suppose so." I couldn't give a precise map reference because I didn't have a map with me as I was familiar with the route. I gave the name of the nearest hamlet. The operator then asked me if I could use 'What3words'. Obviously not, as I gave them a reference to which she responded by informing me that the location was in Oxford. I said I would wait at the hamlet and direct the crew.

Not one, but two ambulances arrived in minutes. This Sunday was obviously a quiet day… for others. Appreciative as I was of their promptness and professionalism, I couldn't help but notice how young they looked. As a head teacher, I had taught pupils who appeared to look this young.

One of them glanced at the motionless individual and instantly stated that there was nothing they could do as he had been dead for a little while. "Looks like a recovery. Stand down the mountain rescue. The police can help us when they've carried out their initial investigations."

After some questioning, I asked if my inability to give the right 'What3words' reference had any negative bearing on this individual's plight. "No, not at all, but at least you had the app. Few do."

"Yes, but if I carried my local map, it would have been useful for an event such as this." Then the policeman gave a useful tip. "When you open the app, pinch the display down to the national map, until you can see a flag and then zoom out again. It recalibrates." All this was taking place as the man's wife appeared on the scene, crying, whilst being consoled by one of the paramedics.

I recounted our morning to the services who could see we were visibly distressed, but were quick to share that these events don't always happen in threes; horrifying I'm sure for any superstitious individual.

Due to the suddenness of John's demise, a post-mortem had to be carried out, thus it was several weeks and into December before the funeral was held. Angie had arranged a double session in the crematorium to avoid a rushed service and to be fair the venue was packed out.

Ironically, Angie said that John didn't really know how much people loved him. His doubts would have been assuredly assuaged judging by the attendance, outpouring of grief and tributes.

Both Geoff and Giles (Smiley) his close, surviving friends who had earlier shared a house with him and Paul, delivered worthy and memorable presentations.

I performed a duet with my nephew George, expecting him to sing solo, thinking the occasion was beyond my vocal capabilities and had resigned myself to instrumental accompaniment only, but strangely the strength of emotion appeared to support my melodic expression. I also told the congregation that John had been a brother to us in the true sense of the word, and he knew we loved him. I also disclosed that he thought I was 'A bit of a tosser at times'… and how did I know this? Because Angie had told me, with a glint in her eye.

Harry delivered a tribute of verse with heartfelt warmth and humour, involving… "An awful swing of fate," with the 'awful swing' reference highlighting John's poor golfing technique. It raised a smile and elicited tears.

Angie insisted that she didn't want to see a mass of black clothing at John's 'send-off', so many came colourfully dressed. "It's what he would have wanted," she said.

Now as already discussed and agreed, Reg can be irreverent or tactless at the best of times, but even Pete and I thought a *comment* to him from one of the guests was a little thoughtless.

"*You* must be getting on a bit now?" To which he replied… "Are you suggesting that I don't bother going home?"

Then Reg delivered the *coup de gras*… "Judging by the way you're dressed today; I'm guessing you've got wooden mirrors at home."

Then Pete pitched in… "He's definitely better looking than you though, isn't he?"

I nodded in agreement.

"You think so?" said the *guest*.

"Oh yes," said Reg (we knew something sabre-like or withering was coming, but it *was* deserved). "At least I haven't got a face like a torn arse!" Job done, we all moved on.

I suppose the one thing that everybody remembered from the service that day was the funeral celebrant. I believe he was of Maltese extraction. A very pleasant man. Not only did he look like Stanley Unwin, but he also sounded uncannily like him; often breaking out into an unconscious, almost bizarre lexicon.

Naturally, of course, Reg was in his element audibly pointing out the similarities, quoting non-stop 'Unwinese' gobbledygook... "Once a polly tighto, a man deffino understanderbold," and of course ending his embarrassing, impromptu performance with a flurry of... "Deep joy, I've falloped over and grazed me knee clabbers, with a prickly on the bumload." Of course, the day's surprises didn't end there.

After responding to the celebrant's farewell at the door, rather like Jeremy Clarkson listening to the incomprehensible dialogue of Gerald Cooper, that is to say with complete confusion, we all set off for the wake breakfast at an 'elite' venue in Gravesend. I, along with the other pallbearers were in one funeral car, whilst the rest of the immediate family members followed in the second vehicle. After twenty minutes or so, the cars drew up outside the hall which was situated next door to a football club called 'Urdu United'(I've changed the name for obvious reasons).

The grounds looked decidedly run down and didn't raise expectations. As we entered the premises, the first sign of disappointment was that of the interior decoration. The stained carpet had certainly taken a battering and had a sticky feel to it. The walls looked 'tired' and the toilets were shockingly uninviting, not to mention unhygienic. Then I saw the catering with the lack of effort and care that had been put into it, and my thoughts turned to Angie who looked saddened, dispirited and embarrassed.

Naturally, everyone was hungry and immediately made their way to the food. *Oh, the food!* I had seen more palatable and presentable cuisine placed into a miner's 'snap' tin. Try to visualise this… thinly sliced, cheap, doughy, 'Value' bread sandwiches between which had been placed a teaspoon of 'Chicken Supreme', with a total absence of butter, crusts left on, *cut into halves* and piled high on a plate without any hint of presentable pride.

Owners of restaurants and function rooms, often labour over their culinary masterpieces to showcase their skills, whilst trying to elicit praise, respect and appeal from the guests. It should be a matter of pride, not an attempt to engage the diner's negative senses. The manager responsible for this catering car crash had to have worked extremely hard to produce such a poor, eye-watering, unstylish attempt at victual virtuosity.

Had it not been for the delightful cakes that Angie had baked, cut up and presented beautifully on plates, one would have thought this was the untouched, cobweb-bedecked wedding breakfast of Miss Havisham from Dickens' masterpiece *Great Expectations*.

Reg stated that the sandwiches brought back the terror of travelling on British Rail, but at least the railway attempted to make them appetising by cutting them into isosceles triangles, before exposing them to sunlight, causing them to curl up… "A bit like John's toes." That went down well—a little better than the fare though, I suspect.

I asked to speak to the manager on Angie's behalf, but of course, he was absent from the crime scene. The poor girl behind the bar couldn't help apologising, but it wasn't her fault or responsibility. She totally agreed with my protestations and promised to relay our disappointment, anger and demand for a refund.

I told Angie that I would pursue the case for her, but despite being upset, she insisted on seeing the owner in person. To her infinite credit, this she did and secured a sizeable return.

Incredibly, she also prepared and took a presentation of sandwiches to show what the catering could and should have looked like.

If anything, one positive outcome of John's shocking and early demise was to bring so many close friends and relatives back under one roof to pledge another coming together to celebrate Ruth and Reg's platinum anniversary the following year. It also became an opportunity for me to distribute (in an Uncle Fred kind of way) copies of my recently released publication 'White Socks and Chalk Dust', at the hotel we were staying the night before. Dad said it would save on the postage and why should I pay out on sending people something they didn't want to read? A fair point but rude.

I wasn't the only person distributing something at the hotel. Somebody had contracted COVID and readily shared the unwanted 'gift'.

After the funeral, rather than hoard or simply stare at and be reminded of her bereavement, Angie started distributing John's possessions to appreciative nephews and other family members. In some cases, she spent time adjusting clothing before handing the articles on. I have several items and derive some comfort from wearing or using them as a means of remembering a wonderful man. Pete and I have pledged to take part in golf tournaments with Geoff and Smiley in memory of John and Paul.

I often think of them when I listen to the tracks they played and loved. In my mind, I can hear their characteristic chuckles, which transport me back to a time when we never considered our mortality. Life can be callous and cruel, but I'm sure someone has said that we can never fully appreciate the extreme feeling of joy, unless we have also suffered the extreme pain of loss.

I frequently think of the surgeon and medical staff who looked after me following the insertion of my two stents and thank them profusely for the bonus and borrowed time they have afforded me. I watch my children, grandchildren and wider family strive and flourish with gratitude and remember to 'contact base' with Mum and Dad for a spirit-raising session of nonsensical banter and meaningful exchanges. Incidentally, I don't call Mum on Mother's Day, nor Dad on Father's Day; wishing instead to contact them at any other time of my choosing, when I'm not reminded to, or when the prices of flowers especially and other gender treats are artificially raised to absurd costs.

Recently, in the March before their platinum celebrations, Reg wanted to take Ruth out for Mother's Day. I suggested that they visit a themed tea shop in Cambridge called 'Carriages of Cambridge'. I mentioned that it had a good write-up. He replied once again in his laconic fashion… "I suppose that'll be the closest we'll get to Claridge's?"

"By the way, when is Mother's Day, Dad?"

"Don't you know? It's nine months after Father's Day!"

I didn't ring John or Paul frequently, but we all enjoyed their company when we got together for family celebrations or events. As John got older, he whinged more, but he certainly didn't have a monopoly on that score. If there were an award for this, I should have won it more than he did. I did notice an upturn in his grumbling whilst playing golf with him and Pete in Lincolnshire, but it's not hard to mourn the loss of our ability to play when we see our sons drive a golf ball one hundred and ninety yards with a *five-iron!* We miss them keenly.

I wish John, Paul and many others could have *batted* for longer, but the Grim Reaper is an accomplished bowler.

# Chapter Thirty-One

The date 27 June 2023 was a memorable milestone in the lives of Reg and Ruth. It was the date of their *seventieth or platinum* wedding anniversary; an incredible achievement and one that was recognised by His Royal Highness King Charles III, or should I say one of his countless administrative employees. I mean, how long would it take the monarch to write 'Charles' on the number of cards received by couples on their seventieth wedding anniversary?

In 2017, it's been suggested that just sixty people in the UK celebrated seventy years of married bliss. I'll make an educated guess that it can't have been too many more in 2023. We'll need access to the most recent census to achieve some idea. Nevertheless, the event must be incredibly rare.

As discussed earlier, Reg and Ruth were aged twenty-two and twenty respectively, when they entered matrimonial 'harmony' in the same year of our late Queen's Coronation. I recently looked at the principal photograph of that joyous occasion with my mother and grandmother both getting wedded to Franklin brothers on the same day and still cannot internalize the unusual proceeding circumstances that led to it. The signing of the register must have been interesting.

"Who naturally would have turned out to be your sister-in-law, was, in fact, your mother-in-law," as well I said to Reg.

"No" he replied, "she was definitely an outlaw!"

When I asked Ruth what the secret was of such a long union she replied, "When things have gone wrong, he's never failed to apologise. Inevitably it's always been his fault anyway!"

Naturally, Barbara wanted to celebrate the anniversary with many friends and relatives at their place and so did Trix because Babs wanted him to. There then began a long torturous run-up to the function with multiple family members involving themselves in its organizing. Many people will have heard of the proverb 'A camel is a horse designed by a committee'.

As quoted by Sir Alec Issigonis, the designer of the original 'Mini' in 1959. The phrase works when incorporating too many conflicting opinions into a single project, but obviously fails when the committee comprises transhumant or nomadic Arab herdsmen. In their case, it's an excellent design. However, spreadsheets, systematic, methodical and meticulous, planning, undoubtedly have their place in the world of business and large events but applying them to a friends and family party discussed over a 'Zoom' platform is as gripping as Alan Carr's handshake.

Despite the breakdowns and wasted time, Babs and Trix decided to invite about one hundred and seventy people to a pig roast. They estimated that a 60-80 kilogram animal would be adequate for their rotisserie and so ordered and paid for that size accordingly. What actually arrived in the back of Angie's car was a 160-kilogram beast, which took four of us a great deal of effort to get out! Cooking this beast was an enormous challenge, requiring us to cut off the legs and trotters before we could fit and suspend it on wires within the gas barbeque. It took twenty-four hours to cook it through and what we didn't eat was stored in a large chest freezer like a dismembered body in a murderer's garage.

Over dinner at Ruth's ninetieth birthday, Reg revealed that he had bought her a beautiful emerald bracelet. As he placed it on her wrist, it sparkled in the light. I told him the present was a romantic gesture and asked if there was a story behind it. "Yes," came the reply, "It was expensive!" When asked if he would like to elaborate on that, he said, "Of course, it was *very* expensive!"

When they are up to it, both Reg and Ruth still go fishing, but now it's usually when Angie and Babs accompany them, just as they have done so with their long-suffering husbands (of Reg I mean not their partners—I think.) John often displayed *comical?* frustration because others didn't take on the responsibility and furthermore, whilst he would have preferred to catch large fish such as carp, Ruth is happy to reel in small fry from the canal and sit 'waiting for Godot'. I'm not sure what his problem was, as I believe most anglers are waiting for something to happen, but it often never does!

I recently joined Reg and Ruth along with Angie, Babs and Trix, during a fishing holiday in Lincolnshire. I enjoyed, as did they, the tranquil surroundings of the lakes and the calming influences of rippling water and birdsong chatter. On one occasion and quite unsolicited, as I sat silently watching her adeptly land a fish, Mum turned to me and said, "Just once."

"Just once what?" I replied, confused. "Just once… you can take him anywhere."

"What prompted that?" I responded with a laugh. "Well, just look at him over on that opposite bank, looking like butter wouldn't melt in his mouth. Any moment now he's going to disturb the fish with a bait ball launched from a catapult, or shatter the silence with a loud emission of wind."

It was equally entertaining when I sat next to Reg on his side of the lake, a bit later. Indeed, after a period of sitting in silence (aimlessly in my opinion) looking at a motionless float, which turned out to be totally ineffective, as the bait had already been filched from the hook by some passing, experienced pond life, Reg informed me that their boiler had recently broken down. "Oh," I remarked with some concern, "have you had it repaired?"

"No son, too costly. I decided to have a heated argument with your mother." He looked towards me with his inimitable facial expression of impishness, which was received with my default expression of incredulity and eye-rolling. "I never know when to believe you."

"Yes, and that's the best part of it, isn't it?"

Reg will also brandish a golf club on occasions and with the help of a buggy, when available, will play nine or eighteen holes—depending on how he feels or the length of others' patience—hitting most shots on the course with a nine-iron. In fairness, he can still swing a reasonable short iron. John understandably, got frustrated at the efficacy of his swing. In truth, John had to endure a great deal since his 'engagement' to the family, but he soon felt palpably better when I reminded him that he never had to live with Reg; a fact that inevitably made him feel measurably better.

I can't help smiling when I think of the occasion at which John introduced his parents and sister to their future in-laws. It was at a party in their large apartment in Stoke Newington. Angie was nineteen at the time and Barbara was seventeen. Throughout the course of the evening, we circulated amongst the guests invited to the London flat, which appeared to be considerably bigger than our humble semi-detached.

An ample buffet had been provided, of which we all availed ourselves. As John was accompanying Reg and me around his home, we espied a couple in a passionate embrace in the hallway. On closer inspection, the fairer sex of the two was identified as Barbara, who looked like she was getting the whole of her face licked by a horse! This should be interesting I thought to myself, and of course, both John and I were not disappointed. Reg leaned over and tapped the unknown fellow on the shoulder, who instantaneously looked around; his face assuming the indignant expression I suspect, of 'Shrek' being interrupted whilst munching into the arse of a one-bite-size rabbit. His mouth was covered in saliva.

As Barbara tried to avert her gaze from the interested and intrigued onlookers, Reg looked him in the eye and said, "Do you want a knife and fork mate, you're definitely making a meal of that! If you're that hungry I suggest you tuck into the buffet that these generous people have provided for you, before setting yourself loose on my daughter again. The heated romantic liaison was extinguished like a jet of $CO_2$ on a raging fire."

Much later after the pair's audience had dispersed, Babs summoned up the courage to confront Reg about making her feel so embarrassed. "I know exactly how you must have felt love. Did you manage to get his name before he tried to eat your face off!"

As mentioned, Reg is still throwing a good dart despite having to continuously support the elbow of his release arm with his other hand because the strength to keep it steady is further dwindling. Since COVID restrictions were eased, he was invited to attend a team practice session, where he took on and beat *three* super-league players in succession! One of the defeated players approached the captain of the club and suggested that Reg might want to join their league. The captain pointed out that Reg had already been down that route having played at county-level for Hertford. "…thing is, he can't get himself around so well now he's ninety-one."

"What? *Ninety-one*?" Reg had been in earshot, "Yes, treble seventeen and double top. If you hit a single, follow up with treble fourteen and double thirty-two. That's percentage darts. Personally, I'd prefer to go out on treble twenty and double top."

The expression of disbelief was apparent on the player's face. He in turn fed this bombshell to his defeated colleagues, who exchanged similar looks of doubt and surprise.

"Are you Captain America?" blurted out one of the losing trio.

"No son, I'm more of your Major Catastrophe!"

"Well, you're definitely an anachronism," came the reply.

"I'm not sure about that, but I probably put the 'knack' in it!"

# Chapter Thirty-Two

Christmas 2023 arrived and although I didn't see either Mum or Dad on the actual day, I arranged to see them at Babs and Trix's old farmhouse with other family members on Boxing Day. However, my arrival was delayed as I went to The Royal Papworth Hospital in Cambridge to see my old friend Ken Rirsch (featured in White Socks and Chalk Dust) who was in for tests following a heart scare. I was very impressed with the design of the hospital, with patients allocated private rooms coming off circular walkways instead of wards. As I arrived, he was talking to Veronica—his late wife Geraldine's sister—(featured in the same book) and her husband.

"Well, this is a pleasant way of avoiding the cooking of Christmas dinner at your house with the rest of the family," I said.

"They're all there now availing themselves of my facilities," Ken replied.

"I'm on my way to see Ruth and Reg following this visit. They both send their regards."

"Well, I'm really glad you didn't bring him with you," said Ken, "because I have to avoid excitement, and my blood pressure is already up!"

I spent an hour or so with Ken and Co and continued my journey to the family celebrations. When I arrived, the merriment was in full flow and to no surprise, Reg was engrossed in watching darts on television. Having embraced, I suggested to him that we might go to a local pub the next day with Harry and have a game of darts. It had been years since we'd played a game together and Harry had never played with his grandfather at all.

"I should very much like that!" said Reg and so it was arranged.

After unsuccessfully finding a board at two locations, we were directed to The George and Dragon in Potton. Inside there was a sizeable group of friends and family playing a game of 'Killer'—a knockout competition.

We sat down and placed our darts on the table in front of us, indicating our interest in playing. Within moments, a friendly guy came over and apologised for the perceived waiting time. After exchanging pleasantries, the chap suggested that Reg join them rather than wait. Harry and I declined the invitation preferring to watch.

There were eight playing in the mini tournament and many others watching on. They were a happy and engaging group, who all showed equal amounts of surprise and disbelief when informed of Dad's age of ninety-two! Similarly, an equal amount of amazement was shown when he beat them all and then saw off all-comers in subsequent games of '301'… double on and off; this including me and Harry who he convincingly white-washed. A young lad by the name of Ryan was playing very well during the 'Killer' knockout until Reg dispatched him with a three-dart finish;

the shock of his dismissal caused him to appeal to his parents in tears.

Unfortunately, he received short shrift from his father who had also been reduced to spectating. Ironically, the only person to beat Reg was Harry during the final game of the evening, by which time Reg was thoroughly knackered and ready for bed. His hosts were incredibly hospitable and insistent that he should return. This was a familiar scene when pub-goers and opposition alike experience his remarkable ability. Even Ryan, after recovering from his earlier exit posted a message on the scoreboard, which simply said, "Go Reg," although I'm not sure whether this was just a request for him to leave!

The date 6 March 2024 brought Reg his 93$^{rd}$ birthday celebrations, and I made arrangements to travel down to see him again. That Wednesday night I took him back to the George and Dragon for a practice session before his up-and-coming semi-final match on the Friday. The manager said they were still talking about Reg's performance on his previous visit. Although not so vociferous about background music and football on television, he still couldn't resist voicing an opinion about not being able to concentrate as well because of it.

On Friday, 8$^{th}$ March, Reg insisted that we leave for the Barnet Social Club where he was to take part in the semi-final of the Hicks Cup by 6:30 pm, stating that he always liked to arrive one hour and a quarter before the match. I asked him if he knew the way, and he said… "Of course, I do." He didn't, but we still arrived with the desired amount of time to spare. It was the first time I'd seen Dad play in a competitive darts match for years.

Upon arrival, Reg produced a leather satchel and took out his real-feather arrows, chalk and spare flights. To be fair I hadn't seen the match shirt he'd put on under his coat until he went up to the oche for a practice. Printed on the back of this T-shirt was 'Reg The Legend'. Now I would have considered it to be the height of boasting, self-indulgence or indeed importance to wear such a claim or slogan, but everyone I spoke to about it said it was a well-deserved and earned present. 'Reg the Lege' was a frequent phrase bandied about that night.

One of Reg's teammates was heard to say to another "How are you, Tony?" Reg instantly interjected audibly... "With a face like he's got, I would have thought it obvious. He's growing a beard to hide as much of it as possible." I turned my bemused expression towards him as Tony reposted, "Do you spend all your time insulting people?"

"No, silly, I've got to sleep on occasions!" Babs once asked him if he ever said anything nice to anyone, and he replied... "Yes, of course, when I look in the mirror!"

I said to him, "You're incorrigible."

"What does that mean?"

"It means you're bloody rude all the time."

"Well, what are they going to do at my age—arrest me? I'd get better food and heating."

"We've only been here twenty minutes and already you're attempting to alienate your entire team!"

"Well, only the ugly ones!"

A guy called Alan came over and introduced himself to me, stating that this was his first season back into competitive darts after twenty years or so. "So, you've had plenty of time to practise then?" said Reg.

I was introduced to some wonderfully friendly and supportive people including a guy named Phil and several Mikes. I met a delightful woman called Lisa Binstead, who had recently and sadly lost her husband and a close friend and partner to Reg following a battle with cancer. Their remarkable sixteen-year-old daughter Charlotte was following in her father's footsteps and had been made team Vice-Captain.

Reg's team won the match thus progressing to the final, with the nonagenarian getting out on a double during one leg and scoring his age in another, much to the delight and raucous cries of his team.

This was obviously a highlight of the evening, but for me, there was an even more memorable moment when I witnessed a sweet interaction between Charlotte and Reg after the former had listened to some advice from her more experienced teammate.

"Thanks, Reg," she replied before leaning forward to embrace him. This was followed by an exchange of banter and laughter. How often do you see individuals engage in such a remarkable and heart-warming act of intimacy, appreciation and friendship when there is such a generational gap? The momentary act of idolatry and guiding support brought an insuppressible tear to my eye.

The evening also afforded me the time to explore Dad's past once again and two extraordinary events in his life were brought to my attention whilst chatting with him that I had not heard before. Firstly, he told of a young German clerical worker employed by the regiment whilst he was serving with the Military Police in Germany. Reg said he was ordered to drive the young girl home on two occasions. On the second trip, he was invited into her home where he was offered tea by her parents.

At some point during this visit, the German parents seriously made an offer to adopt Reg as a son. Thinking this to be yet another joke or manufactured story by him, Reg expressed his appeal at the authenticity of this story. "Why on earth would they wish to make an offer to a soldier of an occupying army?" Reg replied in a serious tone... "Because when I looked at a photograph of their missing son—a pilot in the Luftwaffe—who was shot down in the war, I thought I was looking at myself. They were still grieving terribly."

And there was another revelation: Whilst serving in Germany, a drunken soldier by the name of Harry Fotheringham in the Military Police, pointed a loaded .38 loaded pistol at Reg following a disagreement. "I'll never forget what he said... 'Unlike you, I'm a regular' and I replied yes, a *regular bastard*. You volunteered; I was conscripted! You can't reason with a drunk at the wrong end of a gun, son."

Luckily, a Sergeant Major intervened and subsequently the rating was dismissed from the service. Reg said that it was amazing how his negotiating skills and power of reasoning were improved as he looked down the barrel of a loaded weapon. He also believes this was the moment he lost control of his bowel movements throughout the rest of his life. Obviously, the latter comment is just a reminder of how short his periods of sincerity are!

Reg and I even found time to talk about his school days. I enquired about his memory of events. He said that it was easier to recall incidences that long ago, rather than remembering what Ruth had sent him to the shops for. He remembers sitting in class one day when a supply teacher accused him of talking. I told him that I required pupils to talk in my lessons, as I considered it to be an important part of the learning process. He replied... "Yes, but not during silent reading and this one loved the sound of his own voice anyway. More to the point, I was too busy looking out of the window to talk to anybody. He still blamed me, so I ran out of the classroom and went home.

"The next day, I met up with this temporary member of staff again and he apologised for the mistake and promised to forget the whole issue. However, some little snake reported me to the headmaster, who demanded that I went to his office. Before I did so I gave this little tell-tale a good hiding, which also got back to the headmaster. I was in real trouble and knew I was going to get the cane, so I put a magazine down my trousers to pad out my backside. Sure enough, as I entered his office, he asked me to lean across his desk and hold my hands out. He thrashed the palms of my hands instead!"

# Chapter Thirty-Three

Much more recently, Ruth was talking to some of us about her hip operation and a cataract removal which ended with complications, leaving her with a sub-standard lens and partial sight in her left eye. Under instruction, her doctor was trying to convince her to take blood pressure tablets though she didn't feel it was necessary because she was convinced, if not adamant that her high readings were caused by 'white coat syndrome'. She was conveying the conversation she'd had with the doctor who was desperately trying to persuade her to take the tablets… "Look, Mrs Franklin, will you do me a favour…" at which point, dear Reg interrupted and finished the sentence… "and go to bed with me!" Of course, the sincerity of the moment and Ruth's concentration were broken. In a fit of consternation and exasperation she said, "For God's sake, Reg, I've forgotten where I was."

Dad immediately quipped… "You were in bed with him!" Laughter ensued.

"This is bloody typical of him. He went down to the chemist to get my prescription and when I asked why he didn't come straight back he replied, 'I fell in love with her!'" More raucous laughter ensued.

When I reflect upon all the sixty-six years and some I've known my father, the memories of fun, love, anger, interminable puns, challenges, success, setbacks, loss and indiscretions—including filling the sleeping bags of overnight guests with household items or cakes (and why wouldn't you?)—then the game of darts doesn't present itself as his greatest accomplishment or gift. Like his long-suffering and loving wife, I would place parenting and his 'family-first' mantra, up there in pole position. If longevity is a reward, then without doubt, for them both, it is the return for a lifetime of hard work or devotion to others.

One by one, throughout his magnificent innings (his grandson Harry would approve of that analogy) Reg has witnessed the passing of his parents and fourteen siblings, along with an incalculable number of friends and associates. I for one cannot conceive of the intolerable pain, torment and anguish that is attributed to that onerous title of *Last Man Standing*.

Both Reg and Ruth are terribly proud of all their family, especially the academic, musical and sporting achievements of their children and grandchildren. They love to watch and follow the progress and development of Will's football and Harry's cricket. Like others, they have undoubtedly inherited the size, strength and belief of Reg. It's undeniably quite fitting that I should dedicate the following verse to him, having written it with the attachment I share with him and my son over the game of cricket:

# In Memoriam

As my innings rise
And each run
Is a precious addition
To the latter
You could never quantify
The amount of joy
That you give
When I see you
Score above my age
With each half
And century
I sit back in the shadows
And revel in your glory
When I can no longer
Witness the euphoria
Of your hard-earned
Success
And where I once sat
Now a vacant space
Know in your heart
I should enshroud
Myself in the honour

Of your triumph
Raise a bat
To the memory
Of my pride

As I grow older, I cry more easily and spontaneously at events which emphasise our fragility and weaknesses, but rather more at the joys of our diminishing reunions because inevitably, there will come a time when we won't be around to make light of a crisis or revel in our family gatherings. What would Reg say? "Lighten up son, it may never happen."

Even now, he'll call me on occasions to proudly announce that either in a match he's won or a practice session, he's thrown one or more scores of 'three in a bed'.